SMALL BUSINESS FINANCIAL MASTERY

Comprehensive Guide to Record-Keeping, Compliance, and Growth

Sean Golriz

Copyright © 2024 by TSG Bookkeeping Services. All rights reserved. Printed in United States of America. No part of this book may be used or reproduced in any manner whatsoever without written permission except in the case of brief quotations embodied in critical articles and reviews. For information, please contact TSG Bookkeeping Services.

Although the author and publisher have made every effort to ensure the accuracy and completeness of the information contained in this book, we assume no responsibility for errors, inaccuracies, omissions, or any inconsistency herein. Any slights of people, places, or organizations are unintentional.

Contents

1. Improved Decision Making 5
2. Effective Cash Flow Management 18
3. Ensuring Compliance 48
4. Monitoring Financial Health 71
5. Building Investor Confidence 101
6. Enhancing Operational Efficiency 108
7. Legal Protection 115

The Key Components of Effective Financial Record Keeping 122

Best Practices for Effective Financial Record Keeping 126

The Benefits of Working with a Professional Bookkeeper 128

Introduction

Welcome to **"SMALL BUSINESS FINANCIAL MASTERY, a Comprehensive Guide to Record-Keeping, Compliance, and Growth "**. In today's competitive business landscape, the importance of meticulous financial record-keeping cannot be overstated. This guide is specifically crafted for small business owners like you, who aspire to achieve financial stability, regulatory compliance, and long-term success.

As a small business owner, you wear many hats and juggle numerous responsibilities. Amidst the hustle and bustle of running your business, maintaining organized, up-to-date, and accurate financial records might seem like a daunting task. However, neglecting this critical aspect can lead to severe consequences, including cash flow problems, tax penalties, and missed growth opportunities.

This booklet aims to demystify the process of financial record-keeping, making it approachable and manageable for businesses of all sizes. We will walk you through the fundamental reasons why maintaining impeccable financial records is vital for your business's health and growth. From enhancing decision-making capabilities to ensuring compliance with tax laws, the benefits are manifold.

We understand that every small business is unique, and so are its financial needs. That's why this guide also provides practical tips and best practices tailored to suit a variety of business models. Whether you're just starting out or looking to refine your existing processes, the insights shared here will be invaluable.

Moreover, we'll explore the transformative impact of partnering with a professional bookkeeper. With their expertise, you can streamline your financial management processes, save time, and gain peace of mind, knowing your records are in capable hands. Our goal is to empower you with the knowledge and resources needed to maintain financial integrity, thereby allowing you to focus on what you do best—growing your business.

By the end of this guide, you will have a clear understanding of how to effectively organize and maintain your financial records. More importantly, you'll see the compelling reasons to take action today to ensure your business's financial success. We are here to support you every step of the way, offering customized bookkeeping solutions that fit your specific needs.

Let's embark on this journey together, transforming the way you manage your finances and setting your business up for long-term success. Whether you're looking to establish a solid financial foundation or seeking ways to optimize your current processes, this guide will be your trusted companion. Welcome to a future of financial clarity and business prosperity.

Why Keeping Financial Records Organized Matters

Keeping your financial records organized, up to date, and correct is not just about avoiding tax problems; it's about empowering your business to make informed decisions and plan for the future. Here's why it's essential:

1. Improved Decision Making

Accurate financial records are the foundation of sound decision-making in any business. When your financial data is well-organized and up to date, it becomes a powerful tool that can drive your business forward. Here's a deeper dive into how accurate financial records improve decision-making:

Identify Trends

Spotting patterns and trends in your financial data is crucial for strategic planning. With organized records, you can:

- **Analyze Sales Patterns:** Analyzing sales patterns is a crucial aspect of financial record-keeping and business strategy. It involves examining the data related to sales transactions over a specific period to identify trends and insights that can guide decision-making. Here's a detailed exploration of how to analyze sales patterns and the benefits it brings to your business:

    1. Identifying High-Performing Products or Services

    By analyzing sales patterns, you can determine which products or services are generating the most revenue. Key steps include:

    - **Data Collection:** Gather data on all sales transactions, including product or service names, quantities sold, sales dates, and revenue generated.

- **Sales Reports:** Generate detailed sales reports using accounting software or spreadsheets. These reports should break down sales by product or service, time period, and customer demographics.

- **Trend Analysis:** Look for trends in the data, such as seasonal spikes, consistent best-sellers, or products that perform well in specific markets. Identify the top-performing products or services that consistently drive revenue.

2. Focusing on High-Performing Areas

- Once you have identified the high-performing products or services, you can take strategic actions to maximize their potential. Key strategies include:

- **Inventory Management:** Ensure that you maintain adequate inventory levels of high-performing products to meet customer demand without overstocking.

- **Marketing and Promotion:** Allocate more resources to marketing and promoting high-performing products or services. Use targeted advertising, special offers, and promotions to boost sales further.

- **Product Development:** Invest in developing new features or variants of high-performing products to capitalize on their popularity. Gather customer feedback to understand what improvements or additions would be most valuable.

3. Reconsidering or Improving Low-Performing Products or Services

- Analyzing sales patterns also helps identify products or services that are not performing well. Key steps include:

- **Identifying Low Performers:** Use sales reports to pinpoint products or services with declining sales, low revenue generation, or high return rates.

- **Root Cause Analysis:** Investigate the reasons behind poor performance. Common factors include lack of demand, high competition, poor product quality, inadequate marketing, or misalignment with customer needs.

- **Strategic Decisions:** Decide whether to discontinue, improve, or reposition low-performing products or services. This could involve:

- **Discontinuation:** If a product consistently underperforms with no signs of potential improvement, consider discontinuing it to free up resources for more profitable items.

- **Improvement:** Identify areas for improvement, such as enhancing product quality, updating features, reducing costs, or improving packaging. Conduct market research to understand customer preferences and expectations.

- **Repositioning:** Reposition the product or service in the market by targeting a different customer segment, changing the pricing strategy, or modifying marketing messages.

4. Benefits of Analyzing Sales Patterns

Analyzing sales patterns provides several benefits that can enhance your business's performance and strategic planning. Key benefits include:

- **Informed Decision-Making:** Sales pattern analysis provides data-driven insights that support informed decision-making. It helps you allocate resources effectively, prioritize high-potential areas, and make strategic adjustments.

- **Revenue Growth:** By focusing on high-performing products or services and improving low-performing ones, you can increase overall sales revenue and profitability.

- **Customer Insights:** Understanding which products or services resonate with customers provides valuable insights into their preferences and behaviors. This knowledge can guide product development, marketing strategies, and customer service improvements.

- **Competitive Advantage:** Staying aware of sales trends allows you to respond quickly to market changes, customer needs, and competitive pressures. This agility helps maintain a competitive edge.

- **Operational Efficiency:** Efficiently managing inventory, marketing, and product development based on sales patterns reduces waste and optimizes resource utilization. This contributes to overall operational efficiency.

5. Tools and Techniques for Analyzing Sales Patterns

Several tools and techniques can help you analyze sales patterns effectively. Key methods include:

- **Accounting Software:** Use accounting software with advanced reporting and analytics capabilities. These tools can generate detailed sales reports, track trends, and provide real-time insights.

- **Spreadsheets:** For smaller businesses, spreadsheets can be an effective way to track and analyze sales data. Use formulas, pivot tables, and charts to visualize and interpret the data.

- **Data Visualization Tools:** Utilize data visualization tools like Tableau, Power BI, or Google Data Studio to create interactive dashboards and visual reports. These tools make it easier to identify patterns and trends.

- **Market Research:** Conduct market research to gather additional insights into customer preferences, market trends, and competitive dynamics. Surveys, focus groups, and industry reports can complement your sales data analysis.

- **Performance Metrics:** Track key performance metrics such as sales growth rate, average transaction value, customer acquisition cost, and customer lifetime value. These metrics provide a broader perspective on your sales performance.

- **Understand Seasonal Variations**

    Seasonal variations refer to predictable fluctuations in sales that occur at specific times of the year. These variations can significantly impact your business's operations, planning, and financial health. By identifying and understanding these patterns, you can optimize your inventory management, resource allocation, and marketing strategies to maximize profitability and efficiency.

Identifying Peak and Off-Peak Seasons

To effectively manage seasonal variations, it's crucial to pinpoint when your business experiences peak (high demand) and off-peak (low demand) periods. Key steps include:

- **Data Analysis:** Review historical sales data to identify trends and patterns. Look for recurring increases and decreases in sales at specific times of the year.

- **Sales Reports:** Generate detailed sales reports for different time periods (e.g., monthly, quarterly) to visualize fluctuations. Use graphs and charts to highlight peak and off-peak periods.

- **External Factors:** Consider external factors that may influence seasonal variations, such as holidays, weather changes, and industry-specific events (e.g., back-to-school season, holiday shopping season).

- **Preparing for Fluctuating Demand**

    Once you understand your business's seasonal patterns, you can take proactive steps to manage fluctuating demand effectively. Key strategies include:

Inventory Management:

- **Peak Seasons:** During peak seasons, ensure that you have sufficient inventory to meet increased demand. Stock up on high-demand products in advance to avoid stockouts and missed sales opportunities.

- **Off-Peak Seasons:** In off-peak seasons, reduce inventory levels to prevent overstocking and minimize carrying costs. Focus on selling through existing inventory and avoid placing large orders.

Resource Allocation:

- **Staffing:** Adjust staffing levels to match demand. Hire temporary staff or increase working hours during peak seasons to handle increased customer traffic and sales volume. Reduce staff during slower periods to control labor costs.

- **Marketing and Promotions:**
    - **Peak Seasons:** Ramp up marketing efforts and promotions during peak seasons to capitalize on high demand. Use targeted advertising, special offers, and seasonal campaigns to attract customers.

- **Off-Peak Seasons:** During off-peak periods, focus on maintaining customer engagement through loyalty programs, off-season discounts, and promotions for less popular products or services.

Financial Planning:

- **Cash Flow Management:** Plan your cash flow to accommodate seasonal variations. Ensure that you have sufficient cash reserves to cover expenses during slower periods and manage increased expenses during peak seasons.

- **Budgeting:** Create seasonal budgets that reflect expected revenue and expenses for different times of the year. Adjust your financial plans based on historical data and projected trends.

Benefits of Understanding Seasonal Variations

Understanding and managing seasonal variations in your sales cycle provides several benefits:

- **Improved Customer Satisfaction:** By ensuring that you have the right products in stock during peak seasons, you can meet customer demand promptly, leading to higher customer satisfaction and loyalty.

- **Optimized Inventory Levels:** Effective inventory management reduces the risk of stockouts and overstocking, leading to lower carrying costs and higher profitability.

- **Enhanced Resource Utilization:** Aligning staffing levels and marketing efforts with seasonal demand ensures that resources are used efficiently, reducing operational costs and maximizing returns.

- **Increased Revenue:** Targeted marketing and promotions during peak seasons can boost sales and revenue, while strategic discounts and offers during off-peak periods can maintain customer engagement and drive sales.

- **Better Financial Planning:** Accurate forecasting and budgeting based on seasonal patterns help you manage cash flow, control expenses, and make informed financial decisions.

Tools and Techniques for Managing Seasonal Variations

Several tools and techniques can help you effectively manage seasonal variations:

- **Accounting Software:** Use accounting software to track and analyze sales data, generate reports, and forecast trends. Software solutions can automate data collection and provide real-time insights.

- **Data Visualization Tools:** Leverage data visualization tools like Tableau, Power BI, or

Google Data Studio to create interactive dashboards that highlight seasonal trends and patterns.

- **Inventory Management Systems:** Implement inventory management systems that track stock levels, automate reorder processes, and provide alerts for low stock or excess inventory.

- **Marketing Analytics:** Use marketing analytics tools to measure the effectiveness of seasonal campaigns and promotions. Analyze customer behavior and preferences to refine your marketing strategies.

- **Customer Relationship Management (CRM) Systems:** Utilize CRM systems to track customer interactions, preferences, and purchasing patterns. Use this data to tailor marketing efforts and improve customer engagement.

Evaluate Performance

Regular evaluation of your business strategies is essential for continuous improvement. Accurate financial records enable you to:

- **Measure ROI:** Assess the return on investment (ROI) of various business initiatives, marketing campaigns, and new products. By comparing the costs incurred with the revenue generated, you can determine the effectiveness of these efforts and make informed decisions about future investments.

- **Benchmark Against Goals:** Compare your actual performance against your business goals and objectives. This helps you understand whether you are on track or if adjustments are needed. For example, if your goal was to increase sales by 10% in a quarter and you only achieved 7%, you can analyze why and take corrective actions.

- **Optimize Resource Allocation:** Allocate resources more efficiently by understanding which areas of your business yield the best returns. For example, if a particular product line is highly profitable, you might decide to allocate more budget to marketing it.

Plan for Growth

Accurate financial records provide a solid foundation for forecasting and growth planning. With historical data at your fingertips, you can:

- **Create Financial Projections:** Use past performance data to create realistic financial projections. This includes forecasting sales, expenses, and cash flow, which are critical for budgeting and planning.

- **Set Realistic Growth Targets:** Based on historical trends and current performance, set achievable growth targets. This helps ensure that your goals are ambitious yet attainable, reducing the risk of overextending your resources.

- **Identify Opportunities for Expansion:** Analyze your financial data to identify opportunities for expansion. For example, if a particular market segment shows consistent growth, you might consider investing in new products or services tailored to that segment or expanding your operations geographically.

- **Prepare for Investment:** When seeking investment or financing, detailed financial records are essential. They demonstrate to potential investors or lenders that your business is well-managed and has a clear growth trajectory, increasing your chances of securing funding.

Additional Benefits

- **Enhanced Strategic Planning:** With accurate data, you can develop comprehensive business strategies that are grounded in reality. This includes strategic initiatives like market expansion, product development, and operational improvements.

- **Risk Management:** By regularly reviewing your financial records, you can identify potential risks early. This includes cash flow shortages, rising expenses, or declining sales, allowing you to take proactive measures to mitigate these risks.

- **Improved Operational Efficiency:** Understanding your financial health enables you to streamline operations, reduce waste, and improve overall efficiency. This contributes to better profit margins and a stronger competitive position.

In summary, accurate and organized financial records are invaluable for making well-informed business decisions. They provide the clarity and insights needed to identify trends, evaluate performance, and plan for growth effectively. By leveraging this data, you can steer your business toward sustained success and profitability.

2. Effective Cash Flow Management

Accurate tracking of income and expenses is a cornerstone of effective financial management. It provides a clear picture of a business's financial health, helps in making informed decisions, and ensures compliance with financial regulations. Here's a detailed exploration of how tracking income and expenses benefits your business and how to implement it effectively:

Benefits of Tracking Income and Expenses

1. **Understanding Revenue Streams:**

    - **Identify Income Sources:** Track all sources of income, including sales, services, investments, and other revenue-generating activities. Understanding where your money is coming from is crucial for assessing the sustainability and growth potential of your business.

    - **Analyze Profitability:** By analyzing different revenue streams, you can determine which products, services, or activities are most profitable. This insight helps you focus your efforts and resources on high-performing areas, potentially leading to increased revenue and profitability.

2. **Forecasting:** Accurate tracking of income enables better revenue forecasting. You can predict future cash

flows based on historical data, which aids in budgeting and financial planning.

3. **Categorizing Expenses:**

    - **Expense Breakdown:** Categorize your expenses into specific categories such as rent, utilities, salaries, marketing, supplies, and more. This detailed breakdown helps you see exactly where your money is going and manage your costs more effectively.

    - **Cost Management:** Understanding your expense categories allows you to identify areas where you can cut costs or optimize spending. For example, you might find opportunities to negotiate better terms with suppliers, reduce waste, or implement cost-saving technologies.

    - **Budgeting:** Detailed expense tracking helps in creating more accurate budgets. You can allocate funds more precisely based on historical spending patterns and anticipated future needs.

Implementing Effective Income and Expense Tracking

1. **Use of Accounting Software:**

    - **Automation:** Utilize accounting software to automate the process of tracking income and expenses. Software solutions like QuickBooks, Xero, or FreshBooks can streamline data entry, categorize transactions, and generate reports.

- **Integration:** Integrate your accounting software with other business systems, such as your point-of-sale (POS) system, bank accounts, and payroll services. This ensures that all financial data is captured accurately and in real-time.

2. **Regular Reconciliation:**

    - **Bank Reconciliation:** Regularly reconcile your bank statements with your financial records to ensure that all transactions are accounted for and there are no discrepancies. This helps in identifying errors or fraudulent activities promptly.

    - **Expense Reconciliation:** Reconcile your expense reports with receipts and invoices to ensure that all expenditures are legitimate and properly categorized.

3. **Detailed Record Keeping:**

    - **Income Records:** Maintain detailed records of all income transactions. This includes sales receipts, service invoices, investment returns, and any other income sources. Proper documentation is essential for tracking and verification.

    - **Expense Receipts:** Keep receipts and invoices for all business expenses. Digital copies can be stored in your accounting software or cloud storage for easy access and retrieval.

4. **Periodic Reviews:**

    - **Monthly Reviews:** Conduct monthly reviews of your income and expenses to stay on top of your financial situation. Regular reviews help you spot trends, address issues early, and adjust your financial plans as needed.

    - **Quarterly and Annual Audits:** Perform more comprehensive audits on a quarterly and annual basis to ensure that your financial records are accurate and complete. This is also useful for preparing financial statements and tax filings.

5. **Analysis and Reporting:**

    - **Financial Reports:** Generate detailed financial reports, including income statements, balance sheets, and cash flow statements. These reports provide a comprehensive view of your financial health and performance.

    - **Performance Metrics:** Track key performance metrics such as gross profit margin, net profit margin, and return on investment (ROI). These metrics help you evaluate the effectiveness of your financial strategies and operations.

6. **Budgeting and Forecasting:**

    - **Budget Creation:** Use your tracked income and expense data to create realistic budgets. Allocate resources based on historical trends and future projections to ensure that your business stays within its financial limits.

    - **Forecasting:** Develop financial forecasts to predict future revenue, expenses, and cash flow. Accurate forecasting helps in strategic planning and preparing for potential challenges or opportunities.

Benefits of Accurate Income and Expense Tracking

Accurate tracking of income and expenses is not just about keeping your books in order; it is about empowering your business with the data and insights needed for effective financial management. Here's an expanded explanation of the key benefits:

Enhanced Financial Control

Detailed tracking of income and expenses gives you greater control over your finances. You can make informed decisions based on accurate and up-to-date financial data.

1. **Real-Time Insights:** By regularly updating and reviewing your financial records, you can access real-time insights into your business's financial

health. This allows you to make timely decisions that can positively impact your operations and profitability.

2. **Cash Flow Management:** Understanding your income and expenses helps in managing cash flow effectively. You can predict cash shortages or surpluses and take necessary actions such as securing short-term financing or making investments.

3. **Expense Monitoring:** Keeping a close watch on expenses helps in identifying unnecessary or excessive spending. This enables you to cut costs where possible, ensuring that your financial resources are utilized efficiently.

Improved Profitability

By identifying profitable revenue streams and optimizing expenses, you can improve your overall profitability. This leads to a stronger financial foundation and more opportunities for growth.

1. **Revenue Analysis:** Detailed tracking helps in breaking down revenue by product lines, services, or departments. This allows you to see which areas are most profitable and which ones need improvement or discontinuation.

2. **Cost Reduction:** Analyzing expenses in detail helps in finding cost-saving opportunities. For instance, you might renegotiate contracts with

suppliers, find cheaper alternatives for supplies, or reduce waste.

3. **Margin Improvement:** By understanding the costs associated with each revenue stream, you can adjust pricing strategies to improve profit margins. For example, you can increase prices for high-demand products or services where the market allows.

Compliance and Audit Preparedness

Accurate financial records ensure compliance with tax regulations and make it easier to prepare for audits. Proper documentation can prevent legal issues and penalties.

1. **Tax Compliance:** Keeping accurate records simplifies the process of filing taxes. You can ensure that all deductions are claimed, and income is reported correctly, minimizing the risk of errors and penalties.

2. **Audit Trail:** Well-maintained records provide a clear audit trail, making it easier for auditors to verify your financial transactions. This can streamline the audit process and reduce the likelihood of disputes.

3. **Regulatory Compliance:** Beyond taxes, accurate records help in complying with other regulatory requirements, such as labor laws and industry-specific regulations. This reduces the risk of fines and legal issues.

Strategic Planning

Understanding your financial position enables better strategic planning. You can set realistic goals, develop effective strategies, and allocate resources efficiently.

1. **Goal Setting:** Accurate financial data allows you to set realistic and achievable goals. Whether it's increasing revenue, reducing costs, or expanding operations, having precise data helps in formulating practical objectives.

2. **Resource Allocation:** By knowing exactly where your money is coming from and going, you can allocate resources more effectively. This ensures that capital is directed towards high-impact areas that support your strategic goals.

3. **Long-Term Planning:** Detailed financial records support long-term planning efforts such as business expansion, product development, and market entry strategies. You can create detailed projections and assess the feasibility of different plans.

Investor and Lender Confidence

Accurate financial records enhance the confidence of investors and lenders. They are more likely to invest in or lend to a business that demonstrates financial transparency and stability.

1. **Transparency:** Investors and lenders look for transparency and reliability in financial statements.

Accurate records show that your business is well-managed and financially healthy, increasing their trust and confidence.

2. **Investment Readiness:** Detailed financial records make it easier to prepare business plans and financial statements required for securing investments or loans. This can speed up the funding process and improve your chances of success.

3. **Risk Assessment:** Potential investors and lenders assess the risks associated with your business. Accurate financial records help them understand your business's financial position, cash flow stability, and growth prospects, making your business a more attractive investment or lending opportunity.

Accurate tracking of income and expenses is a powerful tool that offers numerous benefits. It enhances financial control, improves profitability, ensures compliance, supports strategic planning, and boosts investor and lender confidence. By implementing robust financial tracking practices, you can build a strong foundation for your business, make informed decisions, and drive sustainable growth.

Avoiding Shortfalls

One of the main goals of cash flow management is to ensure that your business does not run out of cash. Properly maintained financial records play a crucial role in avoiding cash shortfalls. Here's a detailed explanation of how accurate financial records help you achieve this:

Forecast Cash Flow

Use historical data to predict future cash flow. By projecting your income and expenses, you can anticipate periods of cash shortages or surpluses and plan accordingly.

1. **Historical Analysis:** Reviewing historical financial records allows you to identify trends and patterns in your cash flow. This analysis provides insights into seasonal fluctuations, customer payment behaviors, and recurring expenses.

2. **Cash Flow Projections:** Use historical data to create cash flow projections. These projections estimate future cash inflows and outflows, helping you anticipate when your business might experience cash shortages or surpluses.

3. **Proactive Planning:** With accurate projections, you can take proactive measures to manage your cash flow. For instance, if you anticipate a cash shortage, you can arrange for short-term financing, delay non-essential expenditures, or accelerate receivables collection.

Plan for Large Expenditures

Prepare for significant upcoming expenses, such as equipment purchases, marketing campaigns, or tax payments. Knowing these expenses in advance allows you to allocate funds or seek financing to cover them.

1. **Expense Forecasting:** Accurate financial records help you forecast large upcoming expenses. By knowing when these expenses are due, you can plan your cash flow to ensure that you have enough funds available when needed.

2. **Fund Allocation:** Allocate funds for large expenditures in advance. This might involve setting aside a portion of your revenue each month to build up the necessary amount without disrupting daily operations.

3. **Financing Options:** If a large expenditure exceeds your available cash, knowing about it in advance allows you to explore financing options such as loans, lines of credit, or leasing arrangements. This ensures that you can cover the expense without depleting your cash reserves.

Build a Cash Reserve

Building a cash reserve is a crucial strategy for maintaining the financial health and stability of your business. It provides a buffer against unexpected expenses, economic downturns, and other unforeseen financial challenges. Here's an in-depth look at how to establish and maintain a cash reserve effectively:

Establish a Cash Reserve

Establish a cash reserve to handle unexpected expenses or economic downturns. Knowing your regular cash flow patterns helps you determine how much to set aside without disrupting daily operations.

1. **Analyze Cash Flow Patterns:** Review your historical cash flow data to understand the regular inflows and outflows of your business. This analysis helps you determine how much surplus cash you can allocate to a reserve without affecting your daily operations.

2. **Set Realistic Goals:** Based on your cash flow analysis, set realistic goals for your cash reserve. Typically, it is advisable to have a reserve that can cover at least three to six months of operating expenses.

Emergency Fund

Create an emergency fund to cover unexpected expenses such as equipment repairs, sudden drops in revenue, or unforeseen costs. This fund acts as a financial buffer, providing stability during challenging times.

1. **Identify Potential Risks:** Consider various scenarios that could impact your business, such as equipment breakdowns, natural disasters, or sudden loss of a major client. Understanding these risks

helps in estimating the amount needed for your emergency fund.

2. **Segregate Funds:** Keep your emergency fund separate from your regular operating funds. This ensures that the money is readily available when needed and is not inadvertently used for regular expenses.

3. **Immediate Accessibility:** Ensure that the emergency fund is easily accessible. This might mean keeping it in a high-yield savings account or a money market account, where it can be quickly withdrawn if needed.

Regular Contributions

Use your cash flow patterns to determine a regular contribution amount for your cash reserve. This ensures that you are consistently building up your reserve without significantly impacting your operating cash flow.

1. **Automated Savings:** Set up an automated system to transfer a fixed amount from your revenue into the cash reserve regularly. This could be done weekly, bi-weekly, or monthly, depending on your cash flow cycle.

2. **Percentage-Based Savings:** Consider saving a percentage of your profits or revenue. For example, you might decide to allocate 5-10% of your monthly revenue to the cash reserve.

3. **Adjust Contributions:** Regularly review your cash flow and adjust your contributions as needed. During periods of high revenue, you might increase your contributions, while in lean periods, you might reduce them.

Risk Mitigation

A cash reserve helps mitigate risks associated with economic downturns, market volatility, or sudden changes in your business environment. It provides the financial flexibility to navigate these challenges without severe disruptions.

1. **Economic Downturns:** During economic downturns, having a cash reserve allows you to cover your operating expenses even when your revenue decreases. This can help you avoid layoffs, maintain operations, and potentially take advantage of new opportunities that arise.

2. **Market Volatility:** In industries subject to market volatility, a cash reserve provides the stability needed to withstand fluctuations. It helps in managing periods of low demand or price drops without compromising the long-term health of the business.

3. **Business Environment Changes:** Sudden changes in the business environment, such as new regulations, increased competition, or supply chain disruptions, can be managed more effectively with a

cash reserve. It provides the financial flexibility to adapt to new circumstances without severe disruptions.

Steps to Build and Maintain a Cash Reserve

1. **Assess Financial Health:** Begin by assessing your current financial health. Understand your revenue streams, fixed and variable expenses, and cash flow trends.

2. **Set a Reserve Goal:** Based on your financial assessment, set a specific goal for your cash reserve. Determine the amount needed to cover essential expenses for a defined period, such as three to six months.

3. **Create a Savings Plan:** Develop a savings plan to achieve your cash reserve goal. Decide on the percentage of revenue or profit to be allocated to the reserve and set up automatic transfers.

4. **Monitor and Adjust:** Regularly monitor the progress of your cash reserve. Adjust contributions based on changes in your financial situation or business needs.

5. **Replenish When Used:** If you need to use the cash reserve, prioritize replenishing it as soon as possible to maintain financial security.

Building a cash reserve is a proactive measure to ensure your business can withstand financial shocks and uncertainties. By creating an emergency fund, making regular contributions, and mitigating risks, you enhance your business's resilience and stability. This strategic approach provides peace of mind and the financial flexibility needed to navigate both challenges and opportunities.

Additional Strategies to Avoid Cash Shortfalls

1. **Invoice Promptly:** Ensure that invoices are sent out promptly and follow up on overdue payments. This helps in maintaining a steady cash inflow and reduces the risk of cash shortages.

2. **Expense Management:** Regularly review and manage expenses to ensure they align with your cash flow projections. Avoid unnecessary expenditures and find ways to reduce costs where possible.

3. **Customer Payment Terms:** Consider offering discounts for early payments or setting up payment plans for larger invoices. This can improve cash flow by encouraging quicker payments from customers.

4. **Credit Management:** Carefully manage credit extended to customers. Conduct credit checks on new customers and set credit limits to minimize the risk of non-payment.

5. **Inventory Management:** Optimize inventory levels to balance between meeting customer demand and minimizing cash tied up in stock.

Excess inventory can strain cash flow, while insufficient inventory can lead to lost sales.

Avoiding cash shortfalls is essential for maintaining the financial stability and operational efficiency of your business. Properly maintained financial records are key to achieving this goal. They enable you to forecast cash flow accurately, plan for large expenditures, and build a cash reserve. By implementing these strategies and using accurate financial data, you can ensure that your business has the cash it needs to meet its obligations and seize growth opportunities.

Optimizing Payments

Managing when and how you make and receive payments can significantly impact your cash flow. Accurate financial records are crucial for optimizing payments, as they provide the necessary data to plan and execute effective payment strategies. Here's a detailed explanation of how you can optimize payments:

Schedule Payments Strategically

Plan your payment schedules to align with your cash inflows. For example, if you know that a substantial invoice will be paid by a client at the end of the month, you can schedule your supplier payments shortly after to ensure you have enough cash on hand.

1. **Cash Flow Analysis:** Regularly review your cash flow statements to understand the timing of your cash inflows and outflows. This helps in planning

your payment schedule around periods when you expect to have surplus cash.

2. **Align Payments with Receivables:** If you anticipate receiving significant payments from clients on certain dates, schedule your supplier payments and other significant expenses to follow these dates. This alignment ensures that you have sufficient funds available when making payments.

3. **Avoid Late Fees:** By strategically scheduling your payments, you can avoid late fees and penalties. Ensure that you meet all your financial obligations on time without putting unnecessary strain on your cash flow.

Negotiate Better Terms

With a clear understanding of your financial position, you can negotiate better payment terms with suppliers and clients. This might include extended payment periods or early payment discounts, which can improve your cash flow.

1. **Extended Payment Periods:** Negotiate with suppliers to extend your payment periods. For instance, instead of paying within 30 days, aim for 45 or 60 days. This extension provides more time to gather cash from your sales before making payments.

2. **Early Payment Discounts:** Some suppliers offer discounts for early payments. If your cash flow

allows, take advantage of these discounts to reduce your overall expenses. For example, a 2% discount for paying within 10 days can lead to significant savings over time.

3. **Flexible Payment Plans:** Work with your clients to establish flexible payment plans. This might involve setting up installment payments for large invoices, making it easier for clients to pay and ensuring a steady inflow of cash.

Monitor Accounts Receivable

Keep a close eye on your accounts receivable to ensure timely payments from clients. Implementing a system for regular follow-ups on overdue invoices can help you maintain a steady cash inflow.

1. **Aging Reports:** Generate aging reports regularly to track the status of your accounts receivable. These reports categorize receivables based on how long they have been outstanding, helping you identify overdue invoices that require attention.

2. **Automated Reminders:** Implement an automated system to send reminders to clients about upcoming and overdue payments. Friendly reminders can encourage timely payments and reduce the likelihood of late payments.

3. **Follow-Up Procedures:** Establish a standard procedure for following up on overdue invoices. This might include phone calls, emails, or even

involving a collections agency if necessary. Consistent follow-ups demonstrate that you take timely payments seriously.

4. **Incentives for Early Payment:** Offer incentives to clients for early payments. This could include small discounts or other benefits that encourage clients to pay their invoices ahead of time.

Additional Strategies for Optimizing Payments

1. **Diversify Payment Options:** Provide multiple payment options for your clients, such as credit cards, bank transfers, and online payment systems. This convenience can lead to quicker payments.

2. **Credit Policies:** Establish clear credit policies that outline payment terms and conditions. Communicate these policies to your clients upfront to avoid misunderstandings and delays in payments.

3. **Regular Review:** Regularly review your payment strategies and make adjustments as needed. Economic conditions, client behavior, and business needs can change, so it's essential to stay flexible and adapt your approach.

4. **Payment Schedules for Recurring Expenses:** For recurring expenses like rent, utilities, and payroll, set up automatic payments to ensure they are paid on time without manual intervention. This reduces the administrative burden and helps maintain a positive cash flow.

Optimizing payments is a crucial aspect of effective cash flow management. By scheduling payments strategically, negotiating better terms, and closely monitoring accounts receivable, you can enhance your business's financial stability and flexibility. Accurate financial records are the foundation of these strategies, providing the data needed to make informed decisions and maintain a healthy cash flow. Implementing these practices can lead to improved financial performance, reduced costs, and greater operational efficiency.

Managing Seasonal Variations

Many businesses experience seasonal fluctuations in cash flow, which can significantly impact financial stability. Accurate financial records are essential for managing these variations effectively. Here's a detailed explanation of how to handle seasonal changes in cash flow:

Identify Seasonal Trends

Analyze historical data to identify patterns in your cash flow related to seasonal changes. For example, retail businesses may see higher sales during holidays, while other businesses might have peak seasons at different times of the year.

1. **Historical Data Analysis:** Review your financial records from previous years to identify periods of high and low sales. Look for recurring patterns such

as increased sales during holidays, summer months, or specific industry-related events.

2. **Seasonal Sales Patterns:** Document these patterns and categorize them by month, quarter, or season. Understanding when your business experiences peaks and troughs helps in anticipating cash flow changes.

3. **Market Research:** Conduct market research to understand broader industry trends. This information can provide additional insights into seasonal variations affecting your business and help validate your internal data.

Prepare for Variations

Plan for periods of lower cash flow by saving during high-income periods. This ensures that you have sufficient funds to cover expenses during slower times.

1. **Financial Buffer:** During peak seasons when cash inflows are high, allocate a portion of your profits to a reserve fund. This financial buffer will support your business during off-peak periods when revenue may decline.

2. **Budgeting:** Create a detailed budget that accounts for seasonal fluctuations. Include all fixed and variable expenses and plan for additional costs that may arise during peak seasons, such as increased marketing or inventory purchases.

3. **Cash Flow Projections:** Develop cash flow projections for the entire year, taking into account the identified seasonal trends. This helps in visualizing the periods of surplus and shortage, allowing you to make informed financial decisions.

Adjust Inventory and Staffing

Based on cash flow forecasts, you can adjust your inventory levels and staffing needs to match seasonal demand, avoiding excess inventory or staffing during off-peak periods.

1. **Inventory Management:**

    - **Stock Up for Peak Seasons:** Increase inventory levels in anticipation of higher demand during peak seasons. This ensures you can meet customer demand without stockouts.

    - **Reduce During Off-Peak:** Conversely, reduce inventory levels during slower periods to minimize carrying costs and avoid tying up cash in unsold stock.

    - **Inventory Turnover Analysis:** Regularly analyze inventory turnover rates to understand which products move faster during different seasons. This helps in making informed decisions about inventory purchases.

2. **Staffing Adjustments:**
   - **Hire Temporary Staff:** Consider hiring temporary or part-time staff during peak seasons to handle increased workload. This approach provides flexibility and reduces the financial burden of maintaining a large permanent workforce.
   - **Cross-Training Employees:** Cross-train existing employees to perform multiple roles. This enables you to reassign staff to areas with higher demand during peak seasons without hiring additional personnel.
   - **Flexible Scheduling:** Implement flexible scheduling to adjust labor hours based on demand. For example, increase working hours during busy periods and reduce them during slower times.

Additional Strategies for Managing Seasonal Variations

1. **Marketing Campaigns:** Plan marketing campaigns to boost sales during off-peak periods. Special promotions, discounts, or targeted advertising can help drive traffic and increase revenue when business is typically slower.
2. **Diversification:** Consider diversifying your product or service offerings to balance seasonal fluctuations. For example, if you run a landscaping business,

offering snow removal services in the winter can provide a steady income year-round.

3. **Vendor Relationships:** Maintain strong relationships with your suppliers. Good relationships can lead to favorable payment terms and quicker restocking during peak seasons.

4. **Customer Communication:** Keep your customers informed about seasonal promotions, new products, or changes in operating hours. Effective communication can enhance customer loyalty and encourage repeat business during slow periods.

5. **Technology and Automation:** Use technology to forecast demand and manage inventory efficiently. Automated systems can help track sales patterns, predict future demand, and optimize inventory levels.

Managing seasonal variations in cash flow is critical for maintaining the financial stability of your business. By accurately identifying seasonal trends, preparing for variations, and adjusting inventory and staffing, you can effectively navigate the ups and downs of seasonal demand. Accurate financial records provide the foundation for these strategies, enabling you to make data-driven decisions and ensure your business remains resilient throughout the year. Implementing these practices will help you maintain steady cash flow, reduce financial stress, and capitalize on opportunities during peak seasons.

Enhancing Financial Stability

Effective cash flow management is crucial for the overall financial stability of your business. By maintaining accurate financial records, you can ensure that your business remains solvent, resilient, and capable of seizing growth opportunities. Here's a detailed explanation of how accurate financial record-keeping enhances financial stability:

Reduce Financial Stress

Knowing your financial position and having a clear cash flow plan reduces the anxiety of meeting financial obligations and allows you to focus on growing your business.

1. **Clear Financial Overview:** Accurate financial records provide a comprehensive view of your income, expenses, and cash flow. This clarity helps you understand your financial position at any given time, reducing uncertainty and financial stress.

2. **Timely Payments:** With organized records, you can ensure timely payments to suppliers, employees, and other stakeholders. Avoiding late payments and penalties contributes to financial peace of mind.

3. **Emergency Preparedness:** Maintaining a cash reserve and having a detailed understanding of your cash flow allows you to handle unexpected expenses or financial emergencies without panic.

Knowing you have a safety net reduces stress and allows you to focus on strategic business decisions.

Improve Financial Decision-Making

Make better decisions about investments, expenses, and other financial matters based on a clear understanding of your cash flow situation.

1. **Informed Investments:** Accurate financial records enable you to assess your financial health before making investment decisions. Understanding your cash flow helps you determine whether you can afford to invest in new projects, equipment, or expansion.

2. **Expense Management:** Detailed tracking of income and expenses allows you to identify unnecessary costs and areas where you can cut back without compromising operations. This optimization helps you manage your budget more effectively.

3. **Strategic Planning:** Accurate financial data supports strategic planning. By understanding your cash flow patterns and financial position, you can set realistic goals, develop actionable strategies, and allocate resources efficiently to achieve your business objectives.

Strengthen Creditworthiness

Consistently managing your cash flow well enhances your business's creditworthiness, making it easier to secure loans or attract investors when needed.

1. **Demonstrated Financial Stability:** Lenders and investors look for businesses with strong financial management. Accurate records that show consistent cash flow management demonstrate your business's financial stability and reliability.

2. **Improved Loan Terms:** A well-managed cash flow and strong financial statements can help you secure better loan terms, including lower interest rates and higher credit limits. Lenders are more likely to offer favorable terms to businesses that manage their finances well.

3. **Investor Confidence:** Investors seek businesses that show financial transparency and stability. Accurate financial records enhance investor confidence, making them more likely to invest in your business. Transparent records also facilitate smoother due diligence processes during funding rounds.

Additional Strategies for Enhancing Financial Stability

1. **Regular Financial Reviews:** Conduct regular reviews of your financial records to ensure they are up-to-date and accurate. Regular reviews help you

spot any discrepancies early and make timely corrections.

2. **Cash Flow Forecasting:** Develop cash flow forecasts to anticipate future financial needs and potential shortfalls. This proactive approach allows you to plan for upcoming expenses and ensure you have sufficient funds available.

3. **Diversify Revenue Streams:** Consider diversifying your revenue streams to reduce dependency on a single source of income. Diversification can provide a more stable cash flow and mitigate risks associated with market fluctuations.

4. **Financial Education:** Invest in financial education for yourself and your team. Understanding key financial concepts and best practices helps in making informed decisions and managing the business more effectively.

5. **Leverage Technology:** Use financial management software to automate and streamline financial record-keeping, budgeting, and forecasting. Technology can improve accuracy, save time, and provide real-time insights into your financial health.

Enhancing financial stability through effective cash flow management and accurate financial records is essential for the long-term success of your business. By reducing financial stress, improving decision-making, and strengthening creditworthiness, you can create a solid financial foundation that supports growth and resilience. Implementing these strategies will help you maintain control over your finances, ensure compliance with financial obligations, and attract the confidence of lenders and investors. This stability not only safeguards your business against uncertainties but also positions it for sustainable growth and success.

Tools and Techniques

To enhance cash flow management, consider utilizing:

- **Accounting Software:** Use reliable accounting software to automate tracking and reporting, making it easier to monitor your cash flow in real time.

- **Cash Flow Statements:** Regularly prepare cash flow statements to get a snapshot of your cash inflows and outflows over a specific period.

- **Financial Dashboards:** Implement financial dashboards that provide at-a-glance views of your cash flow, helping you quickly identify and address issues.

In summary, effective cash flow management is essential for maintaining the financial health of your business. By keeping accurate financial records, you can track income and expenses, avoid cash shortfalls, optimize payments, manage seasonal variations, and enhance overall financial stability. These practices enable you to navigate the challenges of running a business and seize opportunities for growth and expansion.

3. Ensuring Compliance

Ensuring compliance with tax regulations and other legal requirements is a fundamental aspect of running a successful business. Well-organized and accurate financial records play a crucial role in this process. Here's a detailed look at how maintaining proper records helps you stay compliant and avoid legal issues:

Prepare Accurate Tax Returns

Accurate and up-to-date financial records are essential for preparing and filing your tax returns correctly. This includes:

1. **Recording All Transactions:**
    - **Comprehensive Documentation:** Ensure that all income and expenses are recorded accurately throughout the year. This provides a complete picture of your financial activities and ensures that nothing is overlooked.
    - **Software and Tools:** Utilize accounting software to record transactions systematically. These tools can automate data entry, reduce errors, and provide a real-time view of your financial status.

2. **Documenting Deductions:**
    - **Receipts and Invoices:** Keep detailed records of all deductible expenses. This includes receipts, invoices, and other

documentation that supports your deductions. Proper documentation maximizes your deductions and reduces the risk of errors.

- **Categorization:** Organize your deductions into categories such as office supplies, travel expenses, and professional services. This organization makes it easier to track and validate deductions during tax filing.

3. **Calculating Taxes Owed:**

    - **Income Tax:** Accurate records enable you to calculate the correct amount of income tax owed. This involves tracking all revenue sources and deducting allowable expenses.

    - **Sales Tax:** For businesses that collect sales tax, maintaining accurate sales records ensures that you remit the correct amount to tax authorities. This includes tracking taxable sales and exempt sales.

    - **Payroll Taxes:** Ensure that payroll records are accurate, including wages, salaries, bonuses, and tax withholdings. This helps in calculating and remitting payroll taxes accurately.

    - **Other Applicable Taxes:** Depending on your business, you may be subject to other taxes such as property tax or excise tax.

Accurate records ensure compliance with these obligations.

Avoid Penalties and Legal Issues

Proper financial record-keeping helps you avoid penalties and legal issues that can arise from non-compliance. This includes:

1. **Timely Filing:**

   - **Deadlines:** Ensure that all tax returns and other required filings are submitted by their respective deadlines. Late submissions can result in penalties and interest charges.

   - **Reminders and Alerts:** Set up reminders and alerts for key filing dates. Accounting software often includes features to help you stay on top of important deadlines.

2. **Accurate Reporting:**

   - **Audit Preparedness:** In the event of an audit, accurate and well-organized records make it easier to provide the necessary documentation and respond to auditor queries. This reduces the risk of penalties and additional scrutiny.

   - **Error Reduction:** Accurate records reduce the likelihood of errors on your tax returns and other filings. This helps prevent discrepancies that could trigger audits or investigations.

3. **Legal Compliance:**

    - **Regulatory Requirements:** Different industries may have specific regulatory requirements related to financial reporting. Accurate records ensure compliance with these industry-specific regulations.

    - **Licenses and Permits:** Maintain records related to business licenses and permits. This documentation is often required for renewals and inspections.

Facilitate Business Operations

Maintaining accurate financial records not only ensures compliance but also facilitates smoother business operations. This includes:

1. **Banking and Financing:**

    - **Loan Applications:** Accurate financial records are essential when applying for business loans or lines of credit. Lenders require detailed financial statements to assess your creditworthiness.

    - **Investor Relations:** Investors often request financial documentation to evaluate the health and potential of your business. Well-organized records enhance transparency and trust.

2. **Internal Management:**

    - **Performance Tracking:** Use financial records to monitor business performance and make informed decisions. This includes tracking revenue growth, expense management, and profitability.

    - **Budgeting and Forecasting:** Accurate records provide the foundation for effective budgeting and financial forecasting. This helps in planning for future growth and managing cash flow.

Ensuring compliance with tax regulations and other legal requirements is critical for the success and longevity of your business. Accurate and well-organized financial records are essential in this process, helping you prepare accurate tax returns, avoid penalties, and facilitate smooth business operations. By maintaining proper records, you can reduce financial stress, improve decision-making, and enhance your business's reputation with lenders, investors, and regulatory authorities. Implementing these practices not only ensures compliance but also positions your business for sustainable growth and success.

Meet Deadlines

Maintaining organized financial records is crucial for staying on top of important tax deadlines and other regulatory requirements. Here's an in-depth explanation of how proper record-keeping helps you meet these deadlines and avoid the associated penalties and disruptions:

Tax Filing Deadlines

Be aware of the various tax filing deadlines throughout the year, including quarterly estimated tax payments, annual income tax returns, and other periodic filings. Organized records make it easier to prepare and file these returns on time.

1. **Annual Income Tax Returns:**

    - **Personal and Business Returns:** Depending on your business structure, you might need to file both personal and business income tax returns. Organized records ensure that all relevant financial data is readily available, making the filing process smoother.

    - **Supporting Documents:** Keep all necessary supporting documents, such as receipts, invoices, and bank statements, organized throughout the year. This minimizes last-minute scrambling and ensures all deductions and credits are properly documented.

2. **Quarterly Estimated Tax Payments:**

    - **Self-Employed and Small Businesses:** Many small businesses and self-employed individuals must make quarterly estimated tax payments to avoid underpayment penalties. Accurate records of your income and expenses help you estimate these payments correctly.

- **Tracking Deadlines:** Use accounting software to set reminders for quarterly estimated tax deadlines, ensuring you never miss a payment.

3. **Sales Tax and Other Periodic Filings:**

    - **Monthly or Quarterly Sales Tax:** Depending on your location and sales volume, you may need to file sales tax returns monthly or quarterly. Keeping sales records organized ensures accurate and timely filings.
    - **Industry-Specific Taxes:** Some businesses are subject to additional taxes, such as excise taxes. Organized records help track these liabilities and ensure timely filing.

Payment Deadlines

Ensure timely payment of taxes to avoid penalties and interest. This includes income tax payments, sales tax remittances, payroll tax deposits, and other tax obligations.

1. **Income Tax Payments:**

    - **Year-End Payments:** At the end of the fiscal year, any remaining tax liabilities must be settled. Organized records help you calculate the exact amount owed, reducing the risk of underpayment or overpayment.

- **Installment Plans:** If you owe a substantial amount, keeping detailed records can help you set up and manage installment plans with the tax authorities.

2. **Sales Tax Remittances:**

   - **Accurate Collection and Remittance:** Ensure you collect the correct amount of sales tax from customers and remit it to the appropriate tax authority on time. Accurate sales records and timely remittance prevent penalties and interest charges.

   - **Reconciliation:** Regularly reconcile your sales tax collected with your remittances to ensure accuracy and compliance.

3. **Payroll Tax Deposits:**

   - **Timely Deposits:** Payroll taxes must be deposited according to a specific schedule, which can be monthly, semi-weekly, or quarterly, depending on your payroll size. Accurate payroll records ensure you make these deposits on time.

   - **Compliance with Withholding Requirements:** Maintain accurate records of employee wages and tax withholdings to comply with federal and state payroll tax requirements.

Compliance with Regulations

Stay compliant with other regulatory requirements, such as licensing, permits, and industry-specific regulations. Proper record-keeping helps you track and meet these obligations.

1. **Licensing and Permits:**

    - **Renewal Reminders:** Keep track of renewal dates for business licenses and permits. Organized records ensure you renew on time, avoiding business interruptions and fines.

    - **Documentation:** Maintain copies of all licenses and permits, along with renewal receipts, in an easily accessible location.

2. **Industry-Specific Regulations:**

    - **Compliance Documentation:** Certain industries have specific regulatory requirements, such as environmental regulations or health and safety standards. Keeping detailed records ensures you can demonstrate compliance during inspections or audits.

    - **Regular Audits:** Conduct internal audits to ensure ongoing compliance with industry regulations. Organized records simplify this process and help identify any areas needing attention.

3. **Other Regulatory Filings:**

    - **Annual Reports:** Many businesses are required to file annual reports with state authorities. Accurate financial and operational records make this filing straightforward.

    - **Corporate Filings:** Corporations may need to file additional documents, such as minutes of meetings or shareholder agreements. Keeping these records organized ensures compliance with corporate governance requirements.

Meeting deadlines for tax filings, payments, and other regulatory requirements is essential to maintaining your business's good standing and avoiding costly penalties. Organized financial records play a critical role in ensuring that you meet these deadlines consistently and accurately. By keeping detailed and up-to-date records, you can streamline your compliance processes, reduce financial stress, and focus on growing your business. Implementing effective record-keeping practices will help you stay on top of your obligations, providing a solid foundation for long-term success and stability.

Respond to Audits

In the event of an audit, having well-maintained financial records is critical. Proper record-keeping can significantly ease the process, ensuring you can provide necessary documentation, demonstrate compliance, and minimize disruption to your business operations. Here's an in-depth explanation of how organized records help you respond effectively to audits:

Provide Documentation

Quickly and easily provide the necessary documentation to auditors. This includes financial statements, tax returns, receipts, invoices, and other supporting documents.

1. **Financial Statements:**

    - **Balance Sheets and Income Statements:** These core financial documents provide a snapshot of your business's financial health. Having them well-organized and up-to-date allows you to present an accurate picture of your finances to auditors.

    - **Cash Flow Statements:** These statements show how cash moves in and out of your business, providing critical insight into your operational efficiency and liquidity.

2. **Tax Returns:**

    - **Income Tax Returns:** Keep copies of your filed income tax returns along with supporting schedules and forms. Organized records ensure you can quickly access any year's return if requested.

    - **Sales and Payroll Tax Returns:** Maintain organized copies of all sales and payroll tax returns, along with records of payments made to tax authorities.

3. **Receipts and Invoices:**
   - **Expense Receipts:** Collect and categorize receipts for all business-related expenses. This documentation supports your deductions and ensures they are valid.
   - **Sales Invoices:** Maintain detailed records of all sales invoices issued. This helps verify your reported income and ensures no revenue is overlooked.

4. **Supporting Documents:**
   - **Bank Statements:** Regularly reconcile your bank statements with your accounting records. This reconciliation helps validate your financial transactions and balances.
   - **Contracts and Agreements:** Keep copies of contracts, leases, and other agreements that impact your financial statements. These documents provide context and support for your financial data.

Demonstrate Compliance

Show that your business has complied with all relevant tax laws and regulations. Organized records provide evidence that you have accurately reported your income and expenses.

1. **Accurate Reporting:**

- **Income Reporting:** Ensure that all sources of income are accurately recorded and reported on your tax returns. This includes sales, interest, and other revenue streams.

- **Expense Deductions:** Properly document all deductible expenses. Organized records provide the necessary evidence to support your deductions, minimizing the risk of disallowance.

2. **Regulatory Compliance:**

    - **Tax Laws and Regulations:** Stay updated on relevant tax laws and regulations affecting your business. Accurate and up-to-date records help you comply with these requirements and demonstrate compliance during an audit.

    - **Industry-Specific Requirements:** Ensure that you meet any industry-specific regulatory requirements. This includes maintaining records related to environmental regulations, health and safety standards, or other industry-specific obligations.

3. **Audit Trails:**

    - **Transaction History:** Maintain a clear audit trail for all financial transactions. This includes detailed records of how transactions were recorded, categorized, and reported.

- **Internal Controls:** Implement and document internal controls to ensure the accuracy and integrity of your financial records. Auditors may review these controls to assess the reliability of your financial data.

Minimize Disruption

Reduce the time and disruption caused by an audit. With everything in order, you can respond to auditors' requests promptly and efficiently, minimizing the impact on your business operations.

1. **Efficient Retrieval:**

    - **Organized Filing System:** Develop an organized filing system, either digital or physical, that allows for quick retrieval of documents. This system should categorize records by type (e.g., income, expenses, taxes) and by date.

    - **Searchable Records:** Use accounting software with robust search capabilities to quickly locate specific transactions or documents.

2. **Proactive Preparation:**

    - **Pre-Audit Review:** Conduct periodic internal reviews of your financial records to ensure they are accurate and complete. This proactive approach helps you identify and address potential issues before an audit occurs.

- **Audit Readiness:** Prepare an audit readiness plan that includes a checklist of documents and records that auditors typically request. Being prepared reduces the time and stress associated with an audit.

3. **Effective Communication:**

    - **Designated Point of Contact:** Assign a knowledgeable point of contact within your business to liaise with auditors. This person should be familiar with your financial records and able to respond to queries efficiently.

    - **Timely Responses:** Provide timely responses to auditor requests. Prompt and complete responses demonstrate your commitment to transparency and compliance, helping to expedite the audit process.

Responding to audits effectively requires well-maintained and organized financial records. By keeping accurate documentation, demonstrating compliance with tax laws and regulations, and minimizing disruption through efficient processes, you can navigate audits smoothly. Proper record-keeping not only eases the audit process but also strengthens your business's overall financial management and stability. Implementing these practices ensures that you are always prepared for an audit, providing peace of mind and allowing you to focus on growing your business.

Maintain Transparency

Transparency in financial reporting is essential for building trust with stakeholders, including investors, creditors, and regulatory authorities. Accurate financial records ensure that your business operations are clear, honest, and credible. Here's an in-depth look at how maintaining transparency through accurate financial records benefits your business:

Financial Statements are Reliable

Produce reliable and transparent financial statements that accurately reflect your business's financial position. This transparency helps build credibility with stakeholders and supports informed decision-making.

1. **Accurate Representation:**
    - **True Financial Health:** Reliable financial statements provide a true and accurate picture of your business's financial health. This includes balance sheets, income statements, and cash flow statements.
    - **Comprehensive Reporting:** Ensure that all aspects of your financial operations are captured in your statements. This comprehensive reporting includes revenue, expenses, assets, liabilities, and equity.

2. **Stakeholder Confidence:**

    - **Investor Trust:** Transparent financial statements build trust with current and potential investors. When investors see accurate and honest reporting, they are more likely to invest in your business.

    - **Creditor Assurance:** Creditors, such as banks and suppliers, rely on your financial statements to assess your creditworthiness. Transparent records help secure better credit terms and improve your borrowing capacity.

3. **Informed Decision-Making:**

    - **Management Decisions:** Accurate financial statements provide management with the data needed to make informed strategic decisions. This includes budgeting, forecasting, and assessing the impact of potential investments or expansions.

    - **Operational Adjustments:** Clear financial records highlight areas of strength and weakness, allowing you to make necessary operational adjustments to improve performance and efficiency.

Regulatory Reporting is Accurate

Ensure that all regulatory reports are accurate and submitted on time. This includes financial disclosures required by regulatory bodies, industry-specific reports, and other mandated filings.

1. **Compliance with Regulations:**
   - **Financial Disclosures:** Many regulatory bodies require businesses to submit detailed financial disclosures regularly. Accurate records ensure that these reports are correct and reflect your business's true financial state.
   - **Industry-Specific Reporting:** Some industries have specific reporting requirements, such as environmental impact reports or health and safety compliance. Proper record-keeping ensures you meet these obligations accurately.

2. **Timely Submissions:**
   - **Meeting Deadlines:** Organized records allow you to prepare and submit regulatory reports on time, avoiding penalties and legal issues. This includes annual financial reports, tax returns, and other required filings.
   - **Proactive Monitoring:** Implement systems to track and remind you of upcoming regulatory deadlines. This proactive approach helps maintain compliance and avoids last-minute rushes.

3. **Auditable Trail:**
   - **Documentation Support:** Accurate records provide the necessary documentation to

support your regulatory filings. This includes invoices, receipts, contracts, and other relevant documents.

- **Audit Readiness:** In case of regulatory audits, having transparent and well-maintained records simplifies the audit process. You can quickly provide auditors with the required information, demonstrating compliance and minimizing disruptions.

Building Long-Term Relationships

1. **Investor and Creditor Relations:**

    - **Consistency and Trust:** Regular, accurate, and transparent financial reporting builds long-term trust with investors and creditors. This trust can lead to more favorable terms, additional funding opportunities, and stronger business relationships.

    - **Enhanced Reputation:** A reputation for financial transparency can enhance your business's standing in the market, attracting new investors and partners.

2. **Customer and Employee Confidence:**

    - **Operational Integrity:** Transparency in financial reporting also builds confidence among customers and employees, ensuring them that your business operates with integrity and stability.

- **Employee Morale:** Employees are more likely to trust and remain committed to a business that is financially transparent and demonstrates stability.

Strategic Planning and Growth

1. **Data-Driven Decisions:**

    - **Resource Allocation:** Transparent financial records provide a clear view of where resources are most needed, enabling better allocation and strategic planning.
    - **Growth Strategies:** With reliable data, you can develop realistic growth strategies, set achievable targets, and measure progress accurately.

2. **Risk Management:**

    - **Identifying Risks:** Clear financial reporting helps identify potential financial risks early, allowing for proactive management and mitigation.
    - **Contingency Planning:** Accurate records support the development of contingency plans to address financial uncertainties or downturns.

Maintaining transparency through accurate financial records is crucial for building and sustaining trust with stakeholders. Reliable financial statements and accurate regulatory reporting demonstrate your business's commitment to honesty, integrity, and compliance. This transparency not only enhances credibility and trust but also supports informed decision-making, strategic planning, and long-term growth. By prioritizing transparency in your financial practices, you lay a strong foundation for your business's stability and success.

Avoid Legal Issues

Maintaining accurate financial records helps you avoid legal issues that can arise from non-compliance with tax laws and regulations. This includes:

- **Penalties and Fines:** Avoid costly penalties and fines for late or inaccurate tax filings. Proper record-keeping ensures that you meet all tax obligations on time and accurately.

- **Legal Disputes:** Reduce the risk of legal disputes with tax authorities and other regulatory bodies. Clear and accurate records provide evidence to support your compliance and protect your business in case of disputes.

- **Regulatory Scrutiny:** Minimize the likelihood of regulatory scrutiny by maintaining transparent and accurate records. Consistent compliance with regulations reduces the chances of triggering audits or investigations.

Best Practices for Ensuring Compliance

To ensure compliance with tax regulations and other legal requirements, adopt the following best practices:

- **Regular Record Updates:** Keep your financial records updated regularly, preferably on a monthly or quarterly basis. This ensures that all transactions are recorded accurately and timely.

- **Use Accounting Software:** Implement reliable accounting software to automate record-keeping and reduce the risk of errors. Many accounting software solutions also offer features to help you stay compliant with tax laws.

- **Hire a Professional:** Consider hiring a professional bookkeeper or accountant to manage your financial records. Their expertise ensures that your records are accurate and compliant with all regulations.

- **Stay Informed:** Keep yourself informed about changes in tax laws and regulations that may affect your business. Regularly consult with a tax professional to stay up to date with new compliance requirements.

- **Implement Internal Controls:** Establish internal controls and procedures to ensure the accuracy and integrity of your financial records. This includes regular reconciliations, audits, and reviews.

In summary, ensuring compliance with tax regulations and other legal requirements is vital for the stability and success of your business. By maintaining accurate and well-organized financial records, you can prepare accurate tax returns, meet deadlines, respond effectively to audits, maintain transparency, and avoid legal issues. Adopting best practices for record-keeping and compliance will help you navigate the complexities of regulatory requirements and focus on growing your business with confidence.

4. Monitoring Financial Health

Monitoring the financial health of your business is crucial for ensuring its long-term sustainability and success. Accurate and up-to-date financial records provide valuable insights into your business's financial status, enabling you to make informed decisions and take proactive measures to maintain and improve your financial health. Here's a detailed exploration of why monitoring financial health is essential and how to effectively do it:

Identify Problems Early

Early identification of financial problems is key to preventing them from escalating into major issues. Accurate financial records help you:

Spot Cash Flow Issues

Regularly review your cash flow statements to identify periods of cash shortages. This early detection allows you to address cash flow problems before they become critical, ensuring that your business can continue to operate smoothly.

1. **Proactive Management:**
    - **Cash Flow Projections:** Create cash flow projections based on historical data and future expectations. This helps in forecasting potential cash shortages and planning accordingly.
    - **Timely Interventions:** Implement measures such as adjusting payment schedules,

securing short-term financing, or reducing discretionary spending to manage cash flow issues effectively.

2. **Operational Adjustments:**

    - **Expense Management:** Identify areas where expenses can be reduced or deferred without impacting core operations. This might include delaying non-essential purchases or negotiating extended payment terms with suppliers.

    - **Revenue Timing:** Accelerate receivables by offering early payment discounts to customers or implementing stricter credit policies to improve cash inflows.

Detect Rising Costs

Monitor your expenses closely to identify any unexpected increases. This enables you to investigate the cause and take corrective actions, such as renegotiating supplier contracts or finding more cost-effective alternatives.

1. **Cost Analysis:**

    - **Detailed Tracking:** Categorize and track all expenses to understand where costs are rising. This includes fixed costs like rent and variable costs like utilities and supplies.

- **Benchmarking:** Compare your expenses against industry benchmarks to identify areas where you may be overspending.

2. **Corrective Actions:**

    - **Supplier Negotiations:** Renegotiate contracts with suppliers to secure better terms or discounts. Consider alternative suppliers if current ones are no longer cost-effective.

    - **Operational Efficiency:** Implement cost-saving measures such as reducing waste, improving process efficiencies, or adopting energy-saving technologies.

Recognize Declining Revenue

Track your revenue trends to spot any downward trends early. By understanding the factors contributing to declining sales, you can implement strategies to boost revenue, such as targeted marketing campaigns or product improvements.

1. **Revenue Analysis:**

    - **Trend Identification:** Analyze sales data to identify trends and patterns, including seasonal variations, product performance, and customer behavior.

    - **Market Analysis:** Conduct market research to understand external factors affecting sales, such as changes in customer preferences, economic conditions, or competitive actions.

2. **Revenue Enhancement:**

    - **Marketing Strategies:** Develop targeted marketing campaigns to attract new customers or retain existing ones. Utilize digital marketing, social media, and promotions to increase visibility and sales.

    - **Product Development:** Innovate and improve your product or service offerings based on customer feedback and market trends. Consider introducing new products or services to meet evolving customer needs.

Key Metrics for Monitoring Financial Health

To effectively monitor your financial health, focus on key financial metrics that provide a comprehensive view of your business's performance:

1. **Profitability Ratios:**

    - **Gross Profit Margin:** Measures the difference between sales and the cost of goods sold. A healthy margin indicates efficient production and pricing strategies.

    - **Net Profit Margin:** Reflects the overall profitability after all expenses. It shows how much profit is generated from total revenue.

2. **Liquidity Ratios:**

    - **Current Ratio:** Assesses your ability to meet short-term obligations with current assets. A ratio above 1 indicates good liquidity.

    - **Quick Ratio:** Similar to the current ratio but excludes inventory. It provides a stricter measure of liquidity.

3. **Leverage Ratios:**

    - **Debt-to-Equity Ratio:** Indicates the proportion of debt used to finance assets relative to equity. A lower ratio suggests a healthier balance sheet with less reliance on debt.

    - **Interest Coverage Ratio:** Measures your ability to pay interest on outstanding debt from operating income. Higher ratios indicate better financial health.

4. **Efficiency Ratios:**

    - **Inventory Turnover:** Indicates how quickly inventory is sold and replaced. Higher turnover suggests efficient inventory management.

    - **Receivables Turnover:** Measures how effectively you collect receivables. Higher ratios indicate efficient credit and collection practices.

5. **Cash Flow Metrics:**
    - **Operating Cash Flow:** Reflects the cash generated from core business operations. Positive cash flow indicates strong operational health.
    - **Free Cash Flow:** Represents the cash available after capital expenditures. It's a key indicator of financial flexibility and investment potential.

Monitoring financial health is a continuous process that requires diligent record-keeping, regular analysis, and proactive management. By maintaining accurate and up-to-date financial records, you gain valuable insights into your business's financial status, enabling you to identify problems early, optimize operations, and make informed decisions. This vigilance ensures your business's long-term sustainability and success, providing a solid foundation for growth and stability.

Measure Profitability

Understanding your profitability is fundamental to assessing your business's financial performance. Accurate financial records enable you to gain detailed insights into various aspects of profitability, which are crucial for making informed decisions and driving your business forward.

Calculate Profit Margins

Profit margins are key indicators of your business's financial health and operational efficiency. There are three primary types of profit margins to consider:

1. **Gross Profit Margin:**

    - **Definition:** This margin measures the difference between sales and the cost of goods sold (COGS). It indicates how efficiently your business is producing or acquiring its products.

    - **Calculation:**

    $$\text{Gross Profit Margin} = \frac{Sales - COGS}{Sales} \times 100$$

    - **Insights:** A higher gross profit margin suggests that your business is effectively managing production costs and pricing strategies. It helps you understand the direct profitability of your products or services.

2. **Operating Profit Margin:**

    - **Definition:** This margin considers operating expenses, providing a clearer picture of profitability by including costs such as salaries, rent, and utilities.

    - **Calculation:**

    $$\text{Operating Profit Margin} = \frac{Operating\ Income}{Sales} \times 100$$

- **Insights:** This metric reflects how well your business is managing its overall operations. A higher operating profit margin indicates efficient cost control and operational effectiveness.

3. **Net Profit Margin:**
    - **Definition:** This margin includes all expenses, such as taxes and interest, offering the most comprehensive view of profitability.
    - **Calculation:**

    $$\text{Net Profit Margin} = \frac{\text{Net Income}}{\text{Sales}} \times 100$$

    - **Insights:** Net profit margin shows the actual profitability after all expenses. A healthy net profit margin signifies that your business is not only generating revenue but also managing its overall expenses effectively.

Analyze Cost Structures

Understanding the structure of your costs is essential for optimizing your business's financial performance. Breaking down costs into fixed and variable expenses helps in various strategic decisions:

1. **Fixed Costs:**

- **Definition:** These are expenses that do not change with the level of production or sales, such as rent, salaries, and insurance.
- **Analysis:** By identifying your fixed costs, you can determine the baseline expenses your business must cover regardless of its sales volume. This helps in budgeting and setting revenue targets.

2. **Variable Costs:**
   - **Definition:** These costs fluctuate with production or sales volume, such as raw materials, direct labor, and utilities.
   - **Analysis:** Understanding variable costs helps in managing production efficiency and pricing strategies. By reducing variable costs, you can directly impact your gross profit margin.

3. **Cost-Volume-Profit (CVP) Analysis:**
   - **Application:** CVP analysis helps in understanding the relationship between cost structures, sales volume, and profitability. It is used to determine the break-even point and the impact of changes in costs or sales on profit.

Evaluate Profit Centers

Identifying and analyzing profit centers within your business allows you to focus on the most profitable areas and make strategic decisions about less profitable segments:

1. **Profit Center Identification:**
   - **Definition:** Profit centers are segments of your business that generate revenue and incur costs, such as specific products, services, departments, or geographical locations.
   - **Analysis:** By evaluating each profit center separately, you can identify which areas are contributing most to your profitability.

2. **High-Profit Segments:**
   - **Focus:** Concentrate on enhancing the operations and marketing efforts of your high-profit segments. Invest in these areas to maximize returns and drive overall business growth.

3. **Low-Profit Segments:**
   - **Improvement or Discontinuation:** For less profitable segments, analyze the reasons for their lower performance. Consider strategies to improve profitability, such as cost reduction, process optimization, or rebranding. If improvement is not feasible, you might decide to discontinue these

segments to focus resources on more profitable areas.

Measuring profitability through accurate financial records is vital for understanding and improving your business's financial performance. By calculating various profit margins, analyzing cost structures, and evaluating profit centers, you gain comprehensive insights into your business's efficiency and areas for improvement. This understanding enables you to make informed decisions, optimize operations, and drive sustained profitability and growth.

Assess Solvency

Solvency is a critical aspect of your business's financial health, indicating your ability to meet long-term financial obligations and sustain operations over time. Accurate financial records play a pivotal role in assessing and maintaining solvency. Here's a detailed look at how to effectively monitor and ensure your business's solvency:

Analyze Debt Levels

Understanding and managing your business's debt is essential for maintaining financial stability:

1. **Review Your Balance Sheet:**
   - **Purpose:** Your balance sheet provides a snapshot of your business's financial position, including assets, liabilities, and equity.

- **Debt Analysis:** By examining your balance sheet, you can assess your total debt levels. This includes both short-term and long-term liabilities, such as loans, bonds, and other financial obligations.

2. **Debt-to-Equity Ratio:**

    - **Definition:** This ratio compares your total liabilities to your shareholders' equity, indicating the relative proportion of debt and equity financing your business uses.

    - **Calculation:**

    $$\text{Debt-to-Equity Ratio} = \frac{Total\ Liabilities}{Shareholders'\ Equity}$$

    - **Insights:** A high debt-to-equity ratio suggests that your business is heavily reliant on debt financing, which can increase financial risk. Managing this ratio helps ensure a balanced and sustainable capital structure.

3. **Debt Management Strategies:**

    - **Actions:** Implement strategies to manage and reduce debt, such as refinancing high-interest loans, negotiating better terms with creditors, and prioritizing debt repayment. This helps improve your financial stability and reduce interest costs.

Monitor Liquidity Ratios

Liquidity ratios provide insights into your business's ability to meet short-term obligations, which is crucial for maintaining day-to-day operations:

1. **Current Ratio:**
    - **Definition:** This ratio measures your ability to pay short-term liabilities with short-term assets.
    - **Calculation:**

    $$\text{Current Ratio} = \frac{\text{Current Assets}}{\text{Current Liabilities}}$$

    - **Insights:** A current ratio above 1 indicates that your business has more current assets than current liabilities, suggesting good short-term financial health. However, a very high ratio may indicate inefficient use of assets.

2. **Quick Ratio (Acid-Test Ratio):**
    - **Definition:** This ratio provides a stricter measure of liquidity by excluding inventory from current assets.
    - **Calculation:**

    $$\text{Quick Ratio} = \frac{\text{Current Assets} - \text{Inventory}}{\text{Current Liabilities}}$$

    - **Insights:** The quick ratio focuses on the most liquid assets, providing a clearer picture of your ability to meet immediate obligations. A quick ratio above 1 is generally considered healthy.

3. **Liquidity Management:**

    - **Actions:** Improve liquidity by optimizing inventory levels, accelerating accounts receivable collections, and managing accounts payable effectively. This ensures that you have sufficient cash flow to cover short-term liabilities.

Plan for Long-Term Obligations

Proactive planning for long-term financial obligations is essential for maintaining solvency and ensuring the sustainability of your business:

1. **Financial Forecasts:**

    - **Purpose:** Use historical financial data and market trends to create financial forecasts. These forecasts help predict future income, expenses, and cash flow.

    - **Benefits:** Accurate forecasting allows you to anticipate and prepare for upcoming financial obligations, ensuring that you have the necessary funds to meet these commitments.

2. **Long-Term Liabilities Management:**

- **Identification:** Identify long-term liabilities such as loan repayments, lease commitments, and retirement benefits.
- **Planning:** Develop a plan to meet these obligations without disrupting your business operations. This includes setting aside funds for loan repayments, negotiating favorable lease terms, and managing pension contributions.

3. **Reserve Funds:**
   - **Establishment:** Establish reserve funds to cover long-term obligations and unexpected expenses. This provides a financial cushion and enhances your business's ability to withstand economic downturns or financial shocks.

Assessing solvency through accurate financial records is crucial for maintaining your business's long-term financial health. By analyzing debt levels, monitoring liquidity ratios, and planning for long-term obligations, you can ensure that your business remains financially stable and capable of sustaining operations. This proactive approach not only mitigates financial risks but also supports informed decision-making and strategic growth.

Enhance Decision-Making

Accurate financial records are the cornerstone of sound strategic decision-making in any business. By continuously monitoring your financial health, you equip yourself with the data needed to make informed choices that drive growth and efficiency. Here's an in-depth look at how maintaining precise financial records enhances decision-making:

Allocate Resources Efficiently

Understanding where to allocate resources is crucial for maximizing business impact and profitability:

1. **Identify Profitable Areas:**

    - **Analysis:** Use financial records to identify which products, services, or business segments are generating the most profit.

    - **Example:** If you discover that a particular product line has significantly higher profit margins, you might allocate more resources to marketing, production, and distribution for that line.

2. **Optimize Expenditures:**

    - **Review Expenses:** Break down your expenses into categories and analyze them to find areas where you can reduce costs without compromising quality or efficiency.

    - **Decision-Making:** Redirect savings from cost-cutting measures into high-impact areas like research and development or customer acquisition.

3. **Resource Allocation:**
    - **Strategy:** Develop strategies for allocating resources that align with your business goals. This might include reallocating funds to underperforming areas that have potential for improvement or scaling up investments in already successful sectors.

Plan for Growth

Financial data is invaluable for developing and implementing growth strategies:

1. **Growth Opportunities:**
    - **Identification:** Use your financial records to spot opportunities for business expansion. This could involve entering new markets, launching new products or services, or acquiring smaller companies.
    - **Example:** If your financial data shows strong performance in a particular region, you might plan to expand your presence there.

2. **Strategic Planning:**
    - **Development:** Create detailed growth plans based on financial insights. This includes setting realistic targets, budgeting for expansion, and forecasting future performance.

- **Implementation:** Allocate resources and develop timelines for achieving growth objectives. Monitor progress and adjust plans as needed based on ongoing financial analysis.

3. **Risk Management:**
    - **Assessment:** Evaluate the risks associated with growth opportunities. Financial records help you understand potential pitfalls and prepare contingency plans.
    - **Mitigation:** Develop strategies to mitigate identified risks, ensuring that growth initiatives are sustainable and do not jeopardize your financial stability.

Evaluate Investment Opportunities

Making informed investment decisions is critical for business success and long-term growth:

1. **Financial Feasibility:**
    - **Assessment:** Use financial records to evaluate the feasibility of potential investments, such as acquiring new equipment, expanding facilities, or launching new products.
    - **Analysis:** Analyze the cost-benefit of each investment opportunity, considering factors

like expected return on investment (ROI), payback period, and impact on cash flow.

2. **Informed Decisions:**

    - **Data-Driven Choices:** Rely on accurate and comprehensive financial data to make well-informed decisions about where to invest. This helps ensure that investments align with your strategic goals and contribute to overall business growth.

    - **Prioritization:** Prioritize investments based on their potential impact and alignment with your business strategy. Focus on high-impact investments that offer substantial long-term benefits.

3. **Funding Strategy:**

    - **Planning:** Develop a funding strategy for your investments, which may include reinvesting profits, securing loans, or attracting investors. Accurate financial records are essential for demonstrating financial stability and attracting external funding.

    - **Execution:** Execute your funding strategy with a clear understanding of your financial position, ensuring that you have sufficient resources to support your investment plans.

Enhancing decision-making through accurate financial records is essential for any business aiming to achieve sustainable growth and operational efficiency. By leveraging precise financial data, you can allocate resources effectively, plan for expansion, and make informed investment decisions. This proactive approach not only strengthens your financial health but also positions your business for long-term success and resilience in a competitive market.

Improve Operational Efficiency

Monitoring your financial health is not just about understanding where your business stands financially; it's also a powerful tool for identifying and implementing improvements that enhance operational efficiency. Accurate financial records provide the insights needed to streamline operations, reduce costs, and ultimately improve your bottom line. Here's a detailed look at how maintaining precise financial records can enhance operational efficiency:

Optimize Inventory Management

Effective inventory management is crucial for maintaining a balance between meeting customer demand and minimizing costs. Accurate financial records help you:

1. **Track Inventory Levels:**
    - **Monitoring:** Regularly track inventory levels to ensure you have the right amount

of stock to meet customer demand without overstocking.

- **Technology Integration:** Use inventory management software that integrates with your financial records to provide real-time data on stock levels and turnover rates.

2. **Analyze Turnover Rates:**

    - **Insights:** Calculate inventory turnover rates to understand how quickly your inventory is being sold and replenished.

    - **Decision-Making:** Use this information to make informed decisions about purchasing and stock levels. High turnover rates indicate strong sales, whereas low turnover rates may suggest overstocking or slow-moving items.

3. **Reduce Carrying Costs:**

    - **Optimization:** Maintain optimal inventory levels to reduce carrying costs associated with storage, insurance, and obsolescence.

    - **Efficiency:** Avoid tying up too much capital in inventory, which can be better utilized elsewhere in the business.

4. **Minimize Stockouts and Excess Inventory:**

    - **Balance:** Strive for a balance that minimizes the risk of stockouts, which can lead to lost sales, and excess inventory, which can lead to markdowns or waste.

- **Forecasting:** Use historical sales data to forecast future inventory needs and adjust your ordering processes accordingly.

Streamline Processes

Operational efficiency often hinges on how well processes are designed and executed. Accurate financial records help you:

1. **Identify Inefficiencies:**
   - **Analysis:** Review your financial records to identify areas where operational costs are higher than expected or where processes are causing delays.
   - **Benchmarking:** Compare your performance metrics against industry standards to pinpoint inefficiencies.

2. **Implement Improvements:**
   - **Redesign Processes:** Streamline workflows and eliminate bottlenecks to enhance productivity and reduce costs.
   - **Technology:** Invest in technology and automation to improve process efficiency. For example, automating repetitive tasks can save time and reduce errors.

3. **Monitor Performance:**
    - **Tracking:** Continuously monitor performance metrics to ensure that implemented improvements are delivering the expected results.
    - **Adjustments:** Make adjustments as needed based on ongoing analysis and feedback from employees and customers.

Control Overhead Costs

Controlling overhead costs is essential for maintaining profitability. Accurate financial records enable you to:

1. **Review Overhead Costs:**
    - **Regular Audits:** Conduct regular audits of your overhead expenses to identify areas where costs can be reduced.
    - **Categorization:** Break down overhead costs into categories such as office expenses, utilities, and administrative costs to gain a clear understanding of where your money is going.

2. **Evaluate Office Expenses:**
    - **Optimization:** Look for ways to optimize office expenses, such as negotiating better lease terms, reducing energy consumption,

or adopting a hybrid work model to decrease office space needs.

- **Supplies Management:** Manage office supplies efficiently by tracking usage and avoiding unnecessary purchases.

3. **Reduce Utilities and Administrative Costs:**

    - **Energy Efficiency:** Implement energy-efficient practices and technologies to reduce utility bills.

    - **Process Improvements:** Streamline administrative processes to reduce labor costs and improve efficiency. This might involve adopting digital tools for tasks like accounting, communication, and document management.

Improving operational efficiency is a continuous process that requires diligent monitoring and analysis of financial data. Accurate financial records provide the foundation for identifying inefficiencies, optimizing processes, and controlling costs. By leveraging these insights, you can enhance your business's productivity, reduce expenses, and ultimately improve your overall profitability. This proactive approach not only strengthens your financial health but also positions your business for sustainable growth and success in a competitive market.

Strengthen Financial Planning

Effective financial planning is a cornerstone of a successful business. Accurate and up-to-date financial data is crucial for making informed decisions and preparing for the future. Monitoring your financial health allows you to create realistic budgets, set financial goals, and prepare for contingencies. Here's an in-depth look at how strengthening financial planning can benefit your business:

Create Realistic Budgets

Developing detailed and realistic budgets is essential for effective financial management. Accurate financial records help you:

1. **Historical Analysis:**
   - **Data Review:** Analyze historical financial data to understand past revenue patterns and expense trends. This analysis provides a solid foundation for creating future budgets.
   - **Pattern Identification:** Identify recurring expenses, seasonal variations in income, and one-time costs that can impact your budgeting process.

2. **Resource Allocation:**
   - **Effective Allocation:** Allocate resources to various departments, projects, or initiatives based on past performance and future projections. This ensures that funds are used

efficiently and align with your business priorities.

- **Prioritization:** Prioritize spending on high-impact areas that drive growth and profitability while keeping discretionary spending in check.

3. **Expense Management:**

    - **Control:** Set spending limits for different categories and monitor actual expenses against budgeted amounts. This helps you stay within your financial means and avoid overspending.

    - **Adjustments:** Make necessary adjustments to your budget throughout the year based on actual financial performance and changing business conditions.

Set Financial Goals

Establishing clear financial goals is crucial for guiding your business toward long-term success. Accurate financial records enable you to:

1. **Goal Setting:**

    - **Specific Targets:** Set specific, measurable, achievable, relevant, and time-bound (SMART) financial goals. Examples include revenue growth targets, profit margins, cost reduction goals, and investment milestones.

- **Benchmarking:** Use industry benchmarks and past performance data to set realistic and challenging financial goals.

2. **Progress Monitoring:**
    - **Regular Reviews:** Regularly review your financial performance against your goals. This helps you track progress and identify areas where you may need to adjust your strategies.
    - **Feedback Loop:** Create a feedback loop where financial performance data informs decision-making and goal adjustments.

3. **Strategic Planning:**
    - **Long-Term Vision:** Develop a long-term strategic plan that aligns with your financial goals. This includes identifying growth opportunities, market expansion, and investment in new products or services.
    - **Resource Alignment:** Ensure that your financial resources are aligned with your strategic priorities and that you are investing in areas that support your long-term vision.

Prepare for Contingencies

Building contingency plans is essential for mitigating financial risks and ensuring business continuity during challenging times. Accurate financial records help you:

1. **Risk Assessment:**
   - **Identify Risks:** Identify potential financial risks, such as economic downturns, market volatility, and unexpected expenses. Understanding these risks helps you develop appropriate contingency plans.
   - **Impact Analysis:** Assess the potential impact of these risks on your financial health and business operations.

2. **Contingency Planning:**
   - **Financial Safety Net:** Create a financial safety net by setting aside funds in a contingency or reserve account. This ensures that you have sufficient liquidity to cover unexpected costs without disrupting your operations.
   - **Scenario Planning:** Develop multiple scenarios for different risk situations and outline specific actions to take in each scenario. This proactive approach helps you respond quickly and effectively to changing circumstances.

3. **Flexibility and Resilience:**
   - **Operational Flexibility:** Maintain operational flexibility to adapt to unforeseen challenges. This includes having flexible staffing arrangements, adjustable inventory levels, and scalable business processes.

- **Resilience Building:** Foster a culture of resilience within your organization by encouraging innovation, continuous improvement, and a proactive approach to problem-solving.

Strengthening financial planning is vital for the long-term success and sustainability of your business. Accurate and up-to-date financial records provide the foundation for creating realistic budgets, setting financial goals, and preparing for contingencies. By leveraging these insights, you can allocate resources effectively, monitor progress toward your goals, and build a financial safety net to navigate challenges. This comprehensive approach to financial planning enhances your business's ability to thrive in a competitive and ever-changing market environment.

Foster Stakeholder Confidence

Transparent and accurate financial reporting builds confidence among stakeholders, including investors, lenders, and employees. Monitoring your financial health demonstrates that your business is well-managed and financially stable. This can lead to:

- **Attracting Investment:** Investors are more likely to invest in a business that demonstrates strong financial health and transparent reporting. Accurate records and regular financial monitoring show that your business is a reliable investment.

- **Securing Financing:** Lenders require detailed financial information to assess your creditworthiness. Regularly monitoring and maintaining accurate financial records increases your chances of securing loans and other forms of financing.

- **Building Employee Trust:** Transparent financial practices and regular updates on the business's financial health foster trust and confidence among employees. This can lead to increased employee engagement and retention.

In summary, monitoring the financial health of your business is essential for identifying problems early, measuring profitability, assessing solvency, enhancing decision-making, improving operational efficiency, strengthening financial planning, and fostering stakeholder confidence. By maintaining accurate and organized financial records, you can gain valuable insights into your business's financial status and make informed decisions to ensure its long-term success and stability.

5. Building Investor Confidence

Building investor confidence is critical for securing funding and support for your business. Investors need to trust that your business is well-managed, financially stable, and capable of delivering returns on their investment. Maintaining accurate and transparent financial records is key to demonstrating this trustworthiness. Here's a detailed exploration of how proper financial record-keeping can build investor confidence:

Transparent Financial Reporting

Transparent financial reporting is the cornerstone of investor confidence. Investors need to see a clear and accurate picture of your business's financial health. Accurate financial records allow you to:

1. **Provide Comprehensive Financial Statements:**

    - Income Statements: Clearly show your revenue, expenses, and profits over a specific period. This helps investors understand how your business generates income and controls costs.

    - Balance Sheets: Display your assets, liabilities, and equity at a particular point in time. This provides insight into your business's financial stability and capital structure.

- Cash Flow Statements: Highlight the flow of cash into and out of your business, detailing operating, investing, and financing activities. Investors use this to assess your liquidity and cash management practices.

2. **Ensure Consistency:**

    - Standard Practices: Adhere to standardized accounting principles and practices (e.g., GAAP or IFRS). This ensures that your financial reports are comparable with those of other businesses, making it easier for investors to evaluate your performance.

    - Historical Data: Maintain consistency in your financial reporting over time. Consistent records help investors identify trends, track growth, and make reliable comparisons year over year. This consistency reassures investors that your business is stable and well-managed.

3. **Offer Detailed Explanations:**

    - Contextual Information: Provide detailed explanations and notes alongside your financial statements. This includes clarifications on significant fluctuations, one-time expenses, extraordinary income, and any accounting policies or changes.

    - Narrative Reports: Use narrative reports to explain the strategic decisions behind the numbers. This transparency helps investors understand the broader context of your financial performance and future prospects.

Demonstrate Financial Health

Investors are more likely to invest in businesses that demonstrate strong financial health. Accurate financial records help you showcase your business's financial stability and growth potential. Key indicators include:

- **Profitability:** Show consistent profitability or a clear path to profitability. Investors want to see that your business can generate profits and sustain growth over the long term.

- **Revenue Growth:** Highlight steady and sustainable revenue growth. This demonstrates that your business is expanding and has the potential to continue growing.

- **Healthy Cash Flow:** Maintain positive cash flow to show that your business can cover its operational costs and reinvest in growth opportunities. Investors need to see that your business can manage its cash effectively.

Evidence of Good Management

Investors look for signs that your business is well-managed and that the management team has a strong handle on financial operations. Accurate financial records provide this evidence by:

- **Showcasing Financial Discipline:** Demonstrate that your business practices sound financial discipline. This includes regular financial reviews, budgeting, and adherence to financial plans. Investors want to see that you are making prudent financial decisions.

- **Highlighting Efficient Operations:** Show that your business operates efficiently and manages costs effectively. Investors are interested in businesses that can maximize profits while minimizing unnecessary expenses.

- **Documenting Strategic Decisions:** Provide records of strategic decisions and their financial impact. This includes investments in new products, market expansions, and other growth initiatives. Investors want to see that your business is proactive and forward-thinking.

Compliance and Risk Management

Investors need assurance that your business complies with all relevant regulations and effectively manages risks. Proper financial records help you demonstrate:

- **Regulatory Compliance:** Show that your business complies with tax laws, industry regulations, and other legal requirements. Accurate records ensure that you meet all obligations and avoid legal issues that could harm your business and investor confidence.

- **Risk Mitigation:** Highlight your risk management practices. This includes maintaining adequate insurance, having contingency plans, and managing financial risks such as currency fluctuations or credit risks. Investors want to know that you are prepared for potential challenges.

Providing Future Projections

Investors are interested in the future potential of your business. Accurate financial records form the basis for reliable future projections, including:

- **Financial Forecasts:** Create detailed financial forecasts based on historical data. This includes projected revenue, expenses, profits, and cash flow. Investors rely on these forecasts to gauge future performance and return on investment.

- **Growth Plans:** Outline your growth plans and strategies, supported by financial data. This includes market expansion, new product development, and other initiatives. Investors want to see that you have a clear and achievable growth strategy.

- **Investment Requirements:** Clearly articulate your investment needs and how the funds will be used. Provide a breakdown of how the investment will drive growth and enhance profitability. Investors need to understand the purpose and expected impact of their investment.

Effective Communication

Building investor confidence also involves effective communication. Regular updates and transparent communication help maintain investor trust. Key practices include:

- **Regular Reporting:** Provide regular financial reports to investors. This includes quarterly and annual financial statements, as well as updates on key performance indicators (KPIs). Regular reporting keeps investors informed and engaged.

- **Open Dialogue:** Maintain an open line of communication with investors. Address their questions and concerns promptly and transparently. This builds trust and shows that you value their input and involvement.

- **Investor Meetings:** Hold regular investor meetings to discuss financial performance, strategic plans, and future outlooks. These meetings provide an opportunity for investors to engage with the management team and gain deeper insights into the business.

Showcasing Achievements

Highlighting your business's achievements and milestones can further build investor confidence. Accurate financial records help you:

- **Document Successes:** Showcase significant achievements, such as revenue milestones, market expansions, and successful product launches. Investors want to see that your business is making progress and achieving its goals.

- **Share Positive Trends:** Highlight positive financial trends, such as increasing profit margins, reduced costs, or improved cash flow. These trends demonstrate that your business is on a positive trajectory.

- **Celebrate Awards and Recognitions:** Share any industry awards, recognitions, or certifications your business has received. These accolades enhance your credibility and demonstrate that your business is recognized for excellence.

In summary, building investor confidence is essential for securing the funding and support needed to grow your business. Maintaining accurate and transparent financial records is key to demonstrating financial health, effective management, compliance, and future potential. By providing comprehensive financial reporting, showcasing achievements, and maintaining open communication, you can build and sustain investor confidence, positioning your business for long-term success and growth.

6. Enhancing Operational Efficiency

Enhancing operational efficiency is a crucial objective for any business seeking to maximize productivity and profitability. Accurate and organized financial records are instrumental in achieving this goal, as they provide the data and insights necessary to streamline processes, reduce costs, and improve overall performance. Here's a detailed exploration of how maintaining proper financial records can enhance operational efficiency:

Streamlining Processes

Efficient processes are the backbone of operational success. Accurate financial records help you:

- **Identify Bottlenecks:** Use financial data to pinpoint areas where workflows are delayed or resources are underutilized. This allows you to address inefficiencies and optimize processes.

- **Standardize Procedures:** Develop standardized procedures for financial tasks such as invoicing, payroll, and expense management. Standardization reduces errors and ensures consistency across operations.

- **Automate Tasks:** Leverage accounting software and automation tools to handle repetitive tasks like data entry, reconciliations, and report generation. Automation saves time and reduces the risk of human error, allowing your team to focus on more strategic activities.

Cost Management

Effective cost management is essential for improving operational efficiency. Accurate financial records enable you to:

- **Track Expenses:** Monitor all business expenses meticulously. This visibility helps you identify unnecessary expenditures and opportunities for cost savings.

- **Analyze Cost Structures:** Break down costs into categories such as fixed and variable expenses. Understanding your cost structure helps you manage expenses more effectively and make informed decisions about pricing and budgeting.

- **Negotiate Better Terms:** Use financial data to negotiate better terms with suppliers and service providers. Demonstrating your financial stability and commitment to long-term relationships can lead to discounts and more favorable contract terms.

Inventory Management

Optimizing inventory management is critical for businesses that deal with physical goods. Accurate financial records support:

- **Inventory Tracking:** Maintain precise records of inventory levels, turnover rates, and stock valuation. This helps you avoid overstocking or stockouts, ensuring that you have the right amount of inventory to meet customer demand.

- **Demand Forecasting:** Use historical sales data to forecast future demand accurately. This enables you to plan inventory purchases more effectively, reducing carrying costs and improving cash flow.

- **Just-In-Time Inventory:** Implement just-in-time (JIT) inventory practices to minimize holding costs and reduce waste. Accurate records allow you to coordinate with suppliers to receive goods only when needed.

Resource Allocation

Efficient resource allocation is key to maximizing productivity. Financial records help you:

- **Identify High-Value Activities:** Determine which activities generate the most revenue and profits. Focus resources on these high-value activities to maximize returns.

- **Optimize Staffing Levels:** Use financial data to analyze labor costs and productivity. This helps you allocate staff more effectively, ensuring that you have the right number of employees in the right roles at the right times.

- **Evaluate Capital Investments:** Assess the financial impact of capital investments, such as new equipment or technology. Accurate records provide the data needed to justify investments and measure their return on investment (ROI).

Performance Measurement

Measuring performance is essential for continuous improvement. Accurate financial records enable you to:

- **Set Performance Metrics:** Establish key performance indicators (KPIs) based on financial data. Common KPIs include revenue growth, profit margins, cost per unit, and return on assets. These metrics provide a clear picture of your business's performance.

- **Benchmark Against Industry Standards:** Compare your financial performance to industry benchmarks. This helps you identify areas where you excel and areas needing improvement.

- **Conduct Regular Reviews:** Schedule regular financial reviews to assess progress toward your goals. Use these reviews to make data-driven decisions and adjust strategies as needed.

Enhancing Customer Satisfaction

Operational efficiency directly impacts customer satisfaction. Accurate financial records help you:

- **Improve Order Fulfillment:** Ensure timely and accurate order processing by maintaining up-to-date records of sales and inventory. This reduces delays and errors in order fulfillment, leading to higher customer satisfaction.

- **Manage Customer Accounts:** Keep detailed records of customer transactions, payments, and communication. This enables you to provide better customer service and resolve issues quickly.

- **Personalize Offers:** Use financial data to analyze customer purchasing patterns and preferences. This allows you to tailor marketing efforts and offers to meet customer needs more effectively.

Reducing Waste

Reducing waste is a key component of operational efficiency. Accurate financial records help you:

- **Monitor Resource Usage:** Track the usage of resources such as materials, energy, and labor. This visibility helps you identify and eliminate wasteful practices.

- **Implement Lean Practices:** Adopt lean management principles to streamline operations and reduce waste. Financial data provides the insights needed to implement and measure the effectiveness of lean initiatives.

- **Optimize Supply Chain:** Use financial records to analyze your supply chain and identify inefficiencies. Streamlining your supply chain can lead to cost savings and faster delivery times.

Strategic Planning

Strategic planning is essential for long-term success. Accurate financial records support:

- **Data-Driven Decision Making:** Base your strategic decisions on reliable financial data. This ensures that your plans are grounded in reality and aligned with your business's financial capabilities.

- **Scenario Analysis:** Conduct scenario analysis to explore the potential impact of different strategies and market conditions. This helps you prepare for various outcomes and make more informed decisions.

- **Long-Term Goals:** Set realistic long-term goals based on historical performance and future projections. Accurate financial records provide the foundation for creating achievable and impactful strategic plans.

Best Practices for Enhancing Operational Efficiency

To enhance operational efficiency through accurate financial records, consider the following best practices:

- **Invest in Technology:** Use modern accounting software and automation tools to streamline financial processes and improve accuracy.

- **Train Staff:** Ensure that your staff is well-trained in financial management and record-keeping practices. Continuous training helps maintain high standards of accuracy and efficiency.

- **Conduct Audits:** Perform regular internal audits to identify and address inefficiencies. Audits help ensure that financial records are accurate and processes are optimized.

- **Implement Continuous Improvement:** Foster a culture of continuous improvement within your organization. Encourage employees to identify and suggest ways to improve processes and reduce waste.

- **Collaborate with Professionals:** Work with professional accountants and financial advisors to ensure that your financial records are accurate and that you are following best practices for efficiency.

In summary, enhancing operational efficiency is vital for maximizing productivity and profitability. Accurate and organized financial records provide the data and insights needed to streamline processes, manage costs, optimize resource allocation, and improve overall performance. By implementing best practices and leveraging financial data, you can achieve greater operational efficiency and drive long-term success for your business.

7. Legal Protection

Maintaining accurate and well-organized financial records provides substantial legal protection for your business. Proper documentation ensures compliance with laws and regulations, helps prevent legal disputes, and can protect your business in the event of an audit or litigation. Here's a detailed exploration of how meticulous financial record-keeping can safeguard your business legally:

Compliance with Laws and Regulations

Ensuring compliance with relevant laws and regulations is a fundamental aspect of legal protection. Accurate financial records help you:

- **Meet Tax Obligations:** Maintain detailed records of all income, expenses, and deductions to accurately prepare and file your tax returns. This helps you avoid penalties and fines for non-compliance with tax laws.

- **Adhere to Industry Regulations:** Many industries have specific regulatory requirements related to financial reporting and record-keeping. Keeping accurate records ensures that you meet these requirements and avoid regulatory penalties.

- **Support Audits:** Be prepared for potential audits by tax authorities or regulatory bodies. Comprehensive financial records provide the necessary documentation to support your reported figures and demonstrate compliance.

Proof of Transactions

Detailed financial records provide proof of all business transactions, which is essential for:

- **Verifying Income and Expenses:** Accurate records validate your reported income and expenses, which is crucial for tax filings, loan applications, and financial statements.

- **Dispute Resolution:** In the event of disputes with customers, suppliers, or business partners, financial records can serve as evidence to support your claims and resolve conflicts.

- **Contract Enforcement:** Maintain records of contracts, agreements, and related financial transactions. These documents provide legal protection in case of breaches or disagreements.

Protection Against Fraud

Fraud prevention and detection are critical for protecting your business. Proper financial record-keeping helps you:

- **Detect Fraudulent Activities:** Regularly review and reconcile your financial records to identify any discrepancies or unusual transactions that may indicate fraud.

- **Implement Internal Controls:** Establish internal controls, such as segregation of duties and authorization procedures, to prevent fraudulent activities. Accurate records support these controls and provide a trail for auditing purposes.

- **Document Financial Policies:** Maintain written policies and procedures for financial transactions and record-keeping. This documentation helps prevent fraud by ensuring that all employees understand and follow established protocols.

Support for Legal Proceedings

In the event of legal proceedings, accurate financial records provide crucial support. They can help you:

- **Demonstrate Financial Health:** Provide evidence of your business's financial health and stability, which can be important in lawsuits, bankruptcy proceedings, or business valuations.

- **Support Insurance Claims:** Maintain records of assets, liabilities, and losses to support insurance claims. Accurate documentation is essential for receiving fair compensation from insurance providers.

- **Provide Legal Defense:** In litigation, financial records can serve as evidence to defend against claims or allegations. Proper documentation strengthens your legal position and helps you present a compelling case.

Employee and Payroll Compliance

Accurate financial records ensure compliance with employment and payroll laws, protecting your business from legal issues related to:

- **Wage and Hour Laws:** Maintain detailed payroll records to ensure compliance with minimum wage, overtime, and other wage and hour regulations. Accurate records help you avoid penalties and lawsuits from employees.

- **Employee Benefits:** Document employee benefits, such as health insurance, retirement plans, and paid time off. This ensures compliance with benefits laws and provides clarity to employees regarding their entitlements.

- **Employment Taxes:** Accurately track and report employment taxes, including federal and state withholding, Social Security, and Medicare taxes. Proper record-keeping helps you meet your tax obligations and avoid penalties.

Intellectual Property Protection

Financial records can also play a role in protecting your intellectual property (IP). They help you:

- **Document IP Expenses:** Track expenses related to developing and protecting your IP, such as patents, trademarks, and copyrights. This documentation supports your IP claims and helps you capitalize on your investments.

- **Valuate IP Assets:** Maintain records of the financial value of your IP assets. Accurate valuation is important for licensing agreements, sales, and legal disputes involving your IP.

- **Enforce IP Rights:** Provide evidence of your IP ownership and the financial impact of any infringement. This documentation is crucial for enforcing your IP rights and seeking damages in legal disputes.

Business Continuity Planning

Accurate financial records are essential for business continuity planning, which helps protect your business from legal and financial risks associated with disruptions. Proper record-keeping supports:

- **Disaster Recovery:** Ensure that your financial records are backed up and accessible in the event of a disaster. This enables you to quickly resume operations and meet legal and contractual obligations.

- **Succession Planning:** Document financial information to facilitate smooth transitions in ownership or management. Clear records help ensure that successors understand the business's financial position and obligations.

- **Risk Management:** Identify and mitigate potential risks to your business. Accurate records provide the data needed to assess risks and develop strategies to protect your business.

Best Practices for Legal Protection Through Financial Records

To maximize legal protection through accurate financial records, consider the following best practices:

- **Maintain Detailed Records:** Keep comprehensive and detailed records of all financial transactions, including receipts, invoices, contracts, and bank statements. Ensure that records are organized and easily accessible.

- **Implement Regular Reviews:** Conduct regular reviews and reconciliations of your financial records. This helps identify discrepancies early and ensures that your records are accurate and up-to-date.

- **Use Accounting Software:** Leverage accounting software to streamline record-keeping and ensure accuracy. Many accounting tools offer features for automating data entry, generating reports, and maintaining audit trails.

- **Secure Your Records:** Protect your financial records by implementing robust security measures, such as encryption, access controls, and regular backups. This safeguards your records from unauthorized access and data loss.

- **Consult Professionals:** Work with professional accountants, auditors, and legal advisors to ensure that your financial records meet legal requirements and best practices. Professional guidance helps you navigate complex regulations and avoid legal pitfalls.

In summary, maintaining accurate and well-organized financial records provides substantial legal protection for your business. Proper documentation ensures compliance with laws and regulations, prevents legal disputes, protects against fraud, supports legal proceedings, ensures employee and payroll compliance, protects intellectual property, and aids in business continuity planning. By implementing best practices and leveraging accurate financial records, you can safeguard your business from legal risks and ensure long-term stability and success.

By understanding and implementing these practices, you set your business up for success, ensuring it runs smoothly, remains compliant, and is prepared for future growth opportunities. Well-organized financial records are not just a necessity; they are a strategic asset that can propel your business forward. Take action today to improve your financial record-keeping and secure a prosperous future for your business.

The Key Components of Effective Financial Record Keeping

Effective financial record-keeping is vital for any business, ensuring accuracy, compliance, and insightful decision-making. Below are the key components that constitute an effective financial record-keeping system:

1. Income Records

Tracking all sources of income is the foundation of understanding your business's financial health. Key practices include:

- **Sales Records:** Maintain detailed records of all sales transactions, including dates, amounts, and customer details. This helps in tracking revenue and understanding sales trends.

- **Other Revenue Streams:** Record any additional sources of income such as interest from savings accounts, rental income, or proceeds from asset sales. Each source should be documented clearly.

- **Documentation:** Keep all sales receipts, invoices, and bank deposit slips. These documents serve as proof of income and are essential for accurate reporting and audits.

2. Expense Records

Detailed records of all business expenses are crucial for managing costs and ensuring accurate tax filings. Key practices include:

- **Expense Categories:** Categorize expenses (e.g., utilities, rent, office supplies) to understand where your money is going. This helps in budgeting and identifying areas for cost savings.

- **Receipts and Invoices:** Retain receipts and invoices for all purchases and payments. This documentation is necessary for tax deductions and verifying expenses.

- **Expense Reports:** Regularly update and review expense reports to monitor spending and ensure that all expenses are recorded accurately and on time.

3. Bank Statements

Reconciling your bank statements with your financial records ensures that all transactions are accurately recorded and helps identify any discrepancies. Key practices include:

- **Monthly Reconciliation:** Perform monthly bank reconciliations to match your financial records with bank statements. This helps in identifying errors, unauthorized transactions, or missed entries.

- **Documentation:** Keep copies of all bank statements and any related documents, such as canceled checks and deposit slips. These are essential for verifying account balances and transactions.

- **Discrepancy Resolution:** Investigate and resolve any discrepancies between your records and the bank statements promptly to maintain accurate financial data.

4. Accounts Receivable and Payable

Managing accounts receivable (money owed to you) and accounts payable (money you owe) is critical for maintaining cash flow and ensuring that your business meets its financial obligations. Key practices include:

- **Invoices:** Issue invoices promptly and track them until they are paid. Use an aging report to monitor overdue invoices and follow up on late payments.

- **Payment Records:** Keep detailed records of all payments made and received, including dates, amounts, and payment methods. This helps in managing cash flow and avoiding disputes.

- **Reconciliation:** Regularly reconcile accounts receivable and payable records with bank statements and accounting records to ensure accuracy.

5. Payroll Records

Accurate payroll records are essential for complying with labor laws and tax regulations. Key practices include:

- **Employee Information:** Maintain up-to-date records of all employees, including personal details, employment contracts, and salary agreements.

- **Wage Records:** Track all wages, salaries, bonuses, and other forms of compensation. Ensure that payroll calculations are accurate and reflect any overtime, deductions, and benefits.

- **Tax Withholding:** Ensure that taxes are withheld correctly from employees' paychecks and remitted to the appropriate tax authorities on time. This includes federal, state, and local taxes, as well as Social Security and Medicare contributions.

- **Payroll Reports:** Generate and review payroll reports regularly to verify accuracy and compliance with legal requirements. Keep these reports for future reference and audits.

6. Tax Records

Organizing all tax-related documents is essential for smooth and timely tax filing. Key practices include:

- **Tax Returns:** Keep copies of all filed tax returns and related documents, including schedules and attachments. These records are important for future reference and potential audits.

- **Tax Payments:** Document all tax payments made, including estimated tax payments and payroll tax deposits. This ensures that you have proof of timely payments and helps avoid penalties.

- **Supporting Documents:** Maintain all supporting documents for tax deductions and credits, such as receipts for business expenses, charitable donations, and investment records. Proper documentation is crucial for substantiating your claims to the tax authorities.

Best Practices for Effective Financial Record Keeping

To ensure that your financial record-keeping system is effective, consider implementing the following best practices:

- **Use Accounting Software:** Leverage accounting software to automate data entry, categorize transactions, and generate reports. This enhances accuracy and efficiency.

- **Set Up a Filing System:** Organize your records using a systematic filing system, whether digital or physical. Ensure that files are labeled clearly and stored securely.

- **Regular Reviews:** Conduct regular reviews of your financial records to identify errors, discrepancies, and areas for improvement. Monthly reviews are recommended to keep records up-to-date.

- **Employee Training:** Train employees involved in financial record-keeping on best practices and the importance of accuracy and compliance. Regular training ensures consistency and reduces errors.

- **Backup Records:** Regularly back up digital records to prevent data loss. Store backups in a secure, off-site location to protect against disasters.

- **Consult Professionals:** Work with professional accountants and bookkeepers to ensure that your financial records meet legal requirements and accounting standards. Professional guidance can help you navigate complex regulations and optimize your record-keeping practices.

In summary, effective financial record-keeping involves accurately tracking income and expenses, regularly reconciling bank statements, managing accounts receivable and payable, maintaining detailed payroll and tax records, and implementing best practices to ensure accuracy, compliance, and efficiency. By focusing on these key components, you can build a robust financial record-keeping system that supports informed decision-making, legal compliance, and the long-term success of your business.

The Benefits of Working with a Professional Bookkeeper

Partnering with a professional bookkeeper brings several benefits to your business:

1. **Accuracy and Expertise:** Professional bookkeepers ensure your records are accurate and up to date.

2. **Time Savings:** Free up your time to focus on running your business while your bookkeeper handles the financial details.

3. **Stress Reduction:** Avoid the stress of managing complex financial tasks and compliance issues.

4. **Financial Insights:** Gain valuable insights and recommendations to improve your business's financial health.

5. **Audit Preparedness:** Be prepared for audits with well-organized and readily available records.

Call to Action

Ready to streamline your financial record-keeping and ensure the success of your business? Here's how we can help:

1. **Free Consultation:** Contact us today to schedule a free consultation and discuss your bookkeeping needs.

2. **Customized Solutions:** We offer tailored bookkeeping services to fit the unique requirements of your business.
3. **Comprehensive Support:** From setup to ongoing management, we're here to support you every step of the way.
4. **Client Success Stories:** Hear from our satisfied clients who have transformed their businesses with our help.

Get Started Today

Don't wait to get your financial records in order. Reach out to us now and discover how professional bookkeeping services can benefit your business. Let's work together to ensure your financial success.

Contact Us:

- **Email:** Info@TSGBookkeeping.com
- **Website:** www. TSGBookkeeping.com

Conclusion

Organized, up-to-date, and accurate financial records are the backbone of a successful small business. By partnering with a professional bookkeeper, you can ensure your records are maintained correctly, giving you the peace of mind and freedom to focus on growing your business. We look forward to helping you achieve financial success.

"Financial Success: The Essential Guide to Organizing and Maintaining Accurate Financial Records for Small Businesses" is your first step towards a well-managed and prosperous business. Let's embark on this journey together and create a stable financial foundation for your enterprise.

TSG Bookkeeping Services

Your Ledger, Our Legacy

Your ledger isn't just a record, it's our commitment to excellence and legacy of trust. With TSG, your books are meticulously managed, reflecting our dedication to precision and integrity, leaving a lasting impact on your business's success!

Schedule Your Discovery Call Today:

www.TSGBookkeeping.com

www.ingramcontent.com/pod-product-compliance
Lightning Source LLC
Chambersburg PA
CBHW031426210526
45464CB00005B/2075